The Decision to Imprison

Sentencing and the Prison Population

Mike Hough

Jessica Jacobson

Andrew Millie

Contents

Acknowledgements   vii

Foreword   viii

Summary   ix

1.   **Introduction**   1
     Background to the study   1
     Aims of the study   3
     Methods   4
     Outline of the report   5

2.   **Accounting for the growth in the prison population**   7
     The prison population   7
     Convictions   10
     Custody rates   12
     Sentence length   13
     Changes in procedure   16
     The use of non-custodial penalties   20
     Summary   21

3.   **Understanding the growth in the prison population**   23
     Has sentencing become more severe?   23
     Has offending increased in seriousness?   28
     Other factors   32
     The rise in the prison population: an overview   33

4.   **Sentencing decisions**   35
     Prison as a last resort   35
     Borderline/cusp cases   36
     The 'unavoidability' of custody   38
     The narratives of sentencing   39

5.	**Alternatives to custody**	**45**
	Sentencers' views of the Probation Service	45
	Do sentencers want feedback on cases?	46
	Does current provision need to be redesigned?	47
	Are more non-custodial options needed?	49
	The sentencer-defendant contract	50
6.	**The political and social context**	**53**
	Pressures from 'the centre'	53
	Pressures from the media and the public	53
	Responding to the pressures	55
7.	**Conclusions: Reducing the prison population**	**59**
	Changing the legal and legislative framework	59
	Extending and improving non-custodial penalties	60
	The climate of opinion about crime and punishment	62
	The political will to restrict prison numbers	64
References		**65**

Acknowledgements

We would like to thank our funders, the Esmée Fairbairn Foundation, who funded the study as part of their Rethinking Crime and Punishment initiative. Without their generosity this study would not have been possible.

A large number of people were very generous with their time. We are grateful to those who helped to get the study off the ground, providing access to our respondents: Sid Brighton, Sally Dickinson, Penny Hewitt, Rachel Lipscomb, Lord Justice Judge and Lord Justice Woolf. We would like to thank all the judges, recorders, district judges and magistrates who took part in the study. They and their staff met the considerable demands we placed on them with forbearance and good humour; but we are especially grateful to them for the spirit of openness with which they approached the study.

Thanks are due to several people who helped us when we were analysing our findings and drafting this report. We would like to thank Rob Allen, Andrew Ashworth, Pat Dowdeswell, Carol Hedderman, Paul Kiff, Rod Morgan, Julian Roberts and Jackie Tombs for reading and commenting on earlier drafts. We would also like to thank Pat Dowdeswell for her help in guiding us through sentencing and prison statistics, and in sharing her own analyses with us. We are grateful to Carrie Buttars and Siân Turner for help with data entry and transcription.

We would like to thank Christine Stewart, formerly Head of Sentencing Policy at the Home Office, for helping the Prison Reform Trust to initiate the study. The study was mounted as a joint enterprise in which the Criminal Policy Research Unit took responsibility for carrying out and reporting the research, and PRT disseminated the results. We are grateful to Geoff Dobson, Kimmett Edgar, Lucy de Lancey, Juliet Lyon, Diana Ruthven and Enver Solomon at PRT. The Trust's staff were consistently constructive and supportive, but at the same time, never failed to respect our independence as researchers.

Mike Hough
Jessica Jacobson
Andrew Millie
July 2003

Mike Hough is Professor of Social Policy and Director of the Criminal Policy Research Unit at South Bank University, where Dr Andrew Millie is a Research Fellow. Dr Jessica Jacobson is an independent consultant.

Foreword

Fifteen years ago when I was Home Secretary the prison population of England and Wales hovered at around the 50,000 mark. Today it is 74,000 and we are told by the Home Office that on present trends it will be over 91,000 by the year 2009. We are well ahead of the rest of western Europe in our readiness to imprison our fellow citizens. 'Ahead' is not quite the right word. The huge expense of this operation is obvious when each new prison place costs £100,000. The usefulness of prisons, even well run prisons, must be questioned when 58% of those so punished re-offend within two years. But our prisons are by no means well run when they are overcrowded as they are today. On the contrary, the gallant efforts which the Prison Service makes to rehabilitate prisoners and set them straight are nullified when the resources of the service are dissipated in shunting prisoners hundred of miles round England and Wales in search of accommodation.

How has this happened and why does it continue? Mike Hough, Jessica Jacobson and Andrew Millie analyse a complicated question in detail but with great clarity. Part, but only part, of the problem lies with the laws on sentencing which Parliament provides. The actual decisions are of course taken by judges and magistrates as they respond, not just to the merits of each case, but to the pressures which they perceive from public opinion and the media.

We in the Prison Reform Trust and other charities in this field take up the continuous challenge of setting out the facts to the public and in particular to those who have the responsibility of passing sentences. We try to deal in facts rather than prejudices, believing that the present trends documented by the Home Office, instead of making us safer, continue to weaken our society. The work done by Mike Hough and colleagues gets behind the headlines to those facts and I am sure that their analysis will be widely studied and welcomed.

Lord Hurd of Westwell
President, Prison Reform Trust

Summary

This study addresses one of the central problems facing contemporary penal policy. The prison population in England and Wales has been rising steeply and progressively. Prisons are overcrowded, budgets are stretched to the limit. Despite this, there has been remarkably little debate about the reasons for this increase, and whether ways can be found of putting a stop to it. This study is intended to go some way to filling the gap.

Key findings

- The adult prison population of England and Wales has grown from 36,000 in 1991 to 62,000 in 2003 – an increase of 71%.

- There are two main reasons why the prison population has grown. Sentencers are now imposing longer prison sentences for serious crimes, and they are more likely to imprison offenders who 10 years ago would have received a community penalty or even a fine.

- Tougher sentencing practice has come about through the interplay of several factors: an increasingly punitive climate of political and media debate about punishment; legislative changes and new guideline judgements; and sentencers' perceptions of changes in patterns of offending.

- The statistics do not lend support to sentencers' beliefs that offenders are becoming more persistent, and committing more serious crimes; however more research is needed on this topic.

- Sentencers consistently say that they send people to prison only as the absolute last resort – either because the offence is so serious that no other sentence is possible; or because the offender's past convictions or failure to respond to past sentences rule out community options.

- Personal mitigation (relating to an offender's condition, circumstances, response to prosecution, and good character) plays a crucial part in cases that result in non-custodial sentences, but are on the borderline with custody.

- Sentencers are not sending people to prison for lack of satisfactory or appropriate community options; they say that they impose community penalties whenever the facts of a case merit it.

- While sentencers are generally satisfied with the quality and range of community sentences, and with the management and enforcement of these sentences, there are widespread concerns that the Probation Service is under-funded.

- Community sentences that carry the provision for review, such as Drug Treatment and Testing Orders, are favoured by sentencers.

- Sentencers say that they are able to resist pressures to 'get tough' from the media and the public, and that it is critically important to do so. At the same time, they feel they have a duty to ensure their sentencing decisions reflect and reinforce the norms of wider society.

Key conclusions

The best way of bringing down the prison population is to issue guidance to sentencers to use imprisonment less often, and where it is used, to pass shorter sentences. Providing a wider range of tougher and more demanding community penalties will probably result in 'net-widening' – where the new sentences are used with offenders who would previously have been fined, or served a conventional community penalty. There is a need to improve sentencers' and the public's awareness of community penalties and their benefits. The courts should make more use of fines, freeing up probation resources and deferring the time when the 'last resort' of imprisonment has to be used. But above all, there needs to be clear, consistent, political leadership in stressing the need to end the uncontrolled rise in the prison population.

The study

At a time when crime has been falling, the prison population in England and Wales has been rising steeply. Today, England and Wales have the highest per capita prison rate in the European Union. Prisons are overcrowded, budgets are stretched to the limit. Despite this, there has been remarkably little debate about the reasons for this increase, and whether ways can be found of putting a stop to it.

Whether to restrict prison numbers is a contentious and thus a political decision. While the case for doing so may be strong, the issue is not explored by this study. Rather, the starting point of the research is the assumption that politicians may wish to curb the use of imprisonment in this country and that if so, they need to know the best ways of doing so. Thus, the study's main aims were to look at what might discourage the use of custody by sentencers, and what might encourage the use of non-custodial alternatives, thereby reversing the rise in the prison population. To this end, the study explored the process by which sentencing decisions are made by judges and magistrates – particularly in relation to cases that are on the borderline between custody and community sentences.

As a preliminary, the study analysed Home Office statistics on convictions and sentencing, and reviewed other relevant academic and policy research.

The core of the study comprised interviews with sentencers. Eleven focus groups were organised for a total of 80 magistrates. Those who took part also completed a detailed questionnaire that asked about sentencing decisions and explored views on non-custodial penalties. One-to-one interviews were carried out with 48 Crown Court judges, recorders and district judges. Interviewees were asked to provide details of four cases which lay on the 'cusp' between custody and community penalties. Five members of the senior judiciary were also interviewed.

Explaining the rise in the prison population

Home Office statistics show that the rise in the prison population cannot be explained simply by greater use of remand, and that it is not the result of more convictions. Two main factors have driven up the prison population: offenders are being imprisoned who previously would have received community penalties; and those who would previously have been sent to prison are being given longer sentences. Between 1991 and 2001, the custody rate for magistrates' courts increased from 5% to 16%. Use of custody by the Crown Court rose from 46% to 64%.

The average length of sentence passed by magistrates' courts was slightly lower in 2001 than it was ten years before. Over the same period the average length of sentences passed by the Crown Court has increased. There has been greater use of long sentences at the expense of middle-range sentences. Within offence categories, sentence length has increased, particularly in relation to convictions for sexual offences and burglary.

Other factors relevant to the prison population include a large increase in the number of defendants found guilty of drugs offences. Some procedural changes have pushed up the prison population, including changes in committal practice and in parole and automatic release. There was a decline in the use of fines, which may have contributed to the prison population since offenders who receive community penalties (rather than fines) early in their criminal careers exhaust the alternatives to prison more rapidly.

Tougher sentences

The increases in custody rates and sentence length strongly suggest that sentencers have become more severe. This greater severity undoubtedly reflects, in part, a more punitive legislative and legal framework of sentencing. Legislation, guideline judgements and sentence guidelines have all had an inflationary effect on sentences passed. At the same time, the climate of political and media debate about crime and sentencing has become more punitive, and is also likely to have influenced sentencing practice.

The five members of the senior judiciary who took part in the study were unanimous in saying that sentencing practice had become more severe, and that this was at least in part a response to political and media pressure on judges and magistrates. Crown Court judges and recorders also tended to refer to external pressures on them to pass tougher sentencing. District judges and magistrates were less likely to talk in terms of sentencing becoming more severe. Magistrates in particular tended to say that sentencing practice had remained unchanged, but that there had been a shift in the nature of cases coming before them.

Whether or not they responded to pressure to pass tougher sentences, almost all of those interviewed were aware of these pressures. Several referred to 'mixed messages' coming from politicians and the senior judiciary, with calls for tougher sentences contradicting calls on sentencers to use prison less.

Perceptions of offending

Sentencers, and magistrates in particular, were more inclined to cite changing patterns of offending, rather than changing sentencing practice, as the underlying cause of the rise in the prison population. While there has been no significant shift in the 'offence mix' of cases coming before the courts, it is possible that statistics on convictions mask some changes in offending behaviour that impact on sentencing.

These changes may be of two main kinds: offenders may be more prolific, and offences within offence categories may be more serious. There is very little statistical support for this, but the views of sentencers were strongly held, and may have some plausibility, given, for example, increases in problematic drug use and in binge drinking. But it may also be that their views have been shaped by the increasingly punitive climate.

Certainly, sentencers' *perceptions* of changing patterns of offending, whatever the extent to which these perceptions are based on actual changes in offending behaviour, are a factor in sentencing practice. The perceptions are thus real in their consequences: if sentencers regard offending behaviour as more serious than hitherto, one might expect them to pass heavier sentences than hitherto.

Sentencing decisions

Sentencers who took part in the study were asked how they had made decisions in cases on the 'cusp' between custodial and non-custodial sentences. It emerged that where a decision was made to impose custody, this was usually based on considerations of the seriousness of the offence, and/or the criminal history of the offender. (The latter played a particularly important part in magistrates' courts.) Hence the use of custody as a 'last resort' had two meanings for sentencers: first, it could refer to the nature of the offence itself; secondly, it could refer to the history of the offender, who might be convicted for a relatively minor offence but was deemed to have run out of options because of the number of past convictions.

In contrast, a wider range of factors were of greatest significance in cusp cases resulting in non-custodial sentences. Issues relating to the present circumstances and condition of the offender were viewed as particularly important in such cases. So too were the offender's response to prosecution (for example, in terms of a show of remorse or willingness to co-operate with the courts) and his or her status as being 'of previous good character'. This emphasis on personal mitigation makes the sentencing process a highly subjective one, in which the sentencer has to make assessments about the attitudes, intentions and capabilities of the offender; assessments which feed judgements about responsibility and culpability.

Sentencers did *not* identify a lack of satisfactory community options as a factor tipping decisions towards custody in cusp cases. According to the analysis of the cusp cases described by the sentencers, only in two of 150 cases that went to custody was a lack of community options cited as a key factor in the sentencing decision. The sentencers stressed that they pass community sentences whenever the facts of a given case make a non-custodial sentence an option.

Community penalties

For the most part, sentencers expressed their satisfaction with the range and content of community sentences available to them. There was strong support for the DTTO, which was felt to be a demanding and potentially constructive sentence. Some sentencers were equally enthusiastic about curfew orders, while others had mixed feelings about these. Many were poorly informed about them.

Sentencers appeared largely satisfied with the work of the Probation Service: in particular, it was observed that the quality of pre-sentence reports and the enforcement of community orders have improved markedly in recent years. However, many also had concerns that under-funding and under-staffing of probation have repercussions for the availability and timeliness of PSRs, and for the supervision of offenders on community sentences.

Some sentencers were poorly informed about the full range of community penalties and about their benefits. Most recognised that the general public were ill-informed about most community penalties. This suggests a need to improve awareness of community penalties both amongst sentencers and amongst the wider public.

Conclusions

Whether the growth of the prison population should be contained is a political decision that falls beyond the boundaries of this study. But if there is some political will to do so, then success in reducing prison numbers will depend on changes both to sentencing practice and to the context in which sentencing is carried out.

One approach that has been tried by successive governments is to provide sentencers with a wider and more attractive range of community penalties. This may go some way to reducing prison numbers. However sentencers in this study did not say that they were using prison for want of adequate non-custodial options. The enhancement of community penalties could simply result in 'net-widening' – where the new sentences are used with offenders who would previously have been fined, or served a conventional community penalty.

Encouraging the use of fines could prove a sensible option. This would relieve pressure on the probation service; in terms of outcomes it could at best deflect some offenders entirely from further offending without resort to imprisonment or community penalties; and at worst it could defer the point in their criminal career where prison becomes inevitable.

The analysis presented here suggests that policies to restrict prison numbers should involve three levels of intervention:

- Adjustment to the legal and legislative framework of sentencing, so as to bring down custody rates and sentence lengths.

- Softening of the climate of political and public opinion on crime and punishment, so that sentencers feel at liberty to make more sparing use of custody, and greater use of the alternatives to custody.

- Improving understanding of the range of non-custodial penalties – including the fine – both among sentencers and the wider public.

However, none of these interventions is likely to meet with much success unless there is clear political will to stop the uncontrolled growth in prison numbers, and visible, consistent, political leadership in stressing the need to do so.

1 Introduction

This study addresses one of the central problems facing contemporary penal policy. At a time when crime has been falling, the prison population in England and Wales[1] has been rising steeply and progressively. Prisons are overcrowded, budgets are stretched to the limit. Despite this, there has been remarkably little debate about the reasons for this increase, and whether ways can be found of putting a stop to it. This study is intended to go some way to filling the gap.

It should be said at the outset that there are several policy options open to a government faced with a rising prison population. Seeking to halt or reverse that rise is not the only option. Other approaches can be adopted: for example, the American criminal justice system has over the last two decades financed and built prisons on an unprecedented scale. In this country too, there has been heavy investment in prison building – though not at the rate of the United States.

This study did *not* set out to answer the question whether increased investment in prisons makes sense as a crime control strategy. Rather, it was premised on the idea that politicians actually want to curb the prison population, and it aims to examine the most effective ways that changes in sentencing can contribute to this. Politicians have expressed concern about rising prison numbers, for example in the White Paper, *Justice for All*[2] (The Stationery Office, 2002). So too have senior officials in the Prison Service and senior members of the judiciary. The financial burden on society of maintaining such a large prison population is heavy: in 2001, the cost per prisoner was £35,939 (Home Office, 2003); and the cost of providing a single new prison place is around £100,000. Finding effective ways of stabilising or reducing the prison population thus seemed a sensible research objective.

There is plenty of research evidence that bears on the question whether restricting prison numbers is a better policy option than investing in more prisons. The consensus amongst criminologists is that crime rates are less responsive to changes in the *severity* of punishment than they are to the *likelihood* of punishment (see von Hirsch *et al.*, 1999, for a review). Certainly prison does not out-perform community penalties in terms of reconviction rates (Prime, 2002). The benefits achieved by prisons in keeping offenders out of circulation – or their 'incapacitation effects' – are also reckoned to be marginal (Goldblatt and Lewis, 1998). However it is not proposed to review this evidence any further here. Although the study is premised on the idea that unchecked growth of the prison population represents a poor investment of finite resources, it is accepted that decisions about the value of extending the use of imprisonment are contentious ones, and thus, properly, political ones. However those politicians who advocate greater use of imprisonment as a crime control strategy – or who are not concerned by rising prison numbers – will find little of use to them in this report.

Background to the study

In 1991, the average daily prison population in England and Wales was 45,897. By 2 May 2003, the prison population had increased by more than half to a total of 73,012. The number of adults in prison (that is, excluding offenders aged 15 to 20) increased at a similar rate from a

---

1 This study restricts itself to sentencing in England and Wales because Scotland and Northern Ireland have separate criminal justice systems.

2 The White Paper identifies the size and cost of the prison population as features of the current sentencing system under the heading 'What is not working'.

daily average of 36,246 in 1991 to 61,971 on 2 May 2003.[3] This rate of increase has been unprecedented, although it follows a general upward trend since the 1940s (Home Office, 2003). It has occurred against a backdrop of gradually declining crime rates since the mid-1990s, according both to recorded crime figures and to the crime counts derived from the British Crime Survey (see Simmons *and colleagues*, 2002).

By October 2002 England and Wales had the highest prison rate in western Europe, at 139 prisoners per 100,000 of population. This compared with a rate of 85 in France and 96 in Germany. Only Portugal, Scotland[4] and Spain, of western European countries, had comparable rates: at 131, 126 and 126 respectively. The prison rate of the United States, in contrast, was much higher, at 686 per 100,000 population. Table 1.1 provides a comparison of prison rates across a selection of European and other countries.

Attempts have been made to compare different countries' use of imprisonment in relation to their crime rates, rather than their overall populations. Such a league table would show Britain in a slightly more favorable light, as its crime rates are relatively high. But the problems in deriving genuinely comparable statistics on this basis are considerable. Research reported in Tonry and Frase (2001) suggested that variations in the imprisonment rate in different countries are to be explained not by variations in crime rates but through differences in sentencing policy and practice.

Table 1.1. Prison rates: International comparisons

Country	Total prison population	Date	Estimated national population	Prison rate (per 100,000 of national population)
USA	1,962,220	31.12.01	286.0m	686
Russian Federation	919,330	1.9.02	144.0m	638
China[1]	1,428,126	Mid-01	1,285.0m	111
Canada	31,624	Mid-01	31.0m	102
England & Wales	72,669	25.10.02	52.4m	139
Portugal	13,384	15.2.02	10.3m	131
Scotland	6,417	25.10.02	5.1m	126
Spain	50,656	31.5.02	40.2m	126
Germany	78,707	30.11.00	82.2m	96
Italy	55,136	1.9.01	58.0m	95
Netherlands	14,968	1.9.01	16.1m	93
France	50,714	1.5.02	59.4m	85
Greece	8,343	1.9.01	10.6m	79
Sweden	6,089	1.10.01	8.9m	68
Northern Ireland	1,058	28.10.02	1.7m	62

Notes (1) Prison figures for sentenced population only

Source: Walmsley (2003)

The size of the prison population creates a range of problems for the Prison Service. Rehabilitation becomes an increasingly difficult aim to achieve as the prison population grows, since efforts to carry out educative and therapeutic work with offenders are hampered by the inevitable problems of overcrowding and the excessive burdens made on prison staff.[5] Prison overcrowding has grown with the rise in the prison population: in 2001, for example,

---

3 Sources: 1991 (Home Office 2003); 2003 (HM Prisons, 2003 www.hmprisonservice.gov.uk/statistics).

4 The Esmée Fairbairn Foundation have funded comparable Scottish research as part of their Rethinking Crime and Punishment Initiative which will be published in 2004.

5 Problems are associated with lack of oversight, lack of purposeful activity and with having to move people from prison to prison. These are exacerbated by staff shortages and sickness rates. See also Levenson (2002).

11,204 prisoners were held two to a cell designed for one (Home Office, 2003). In response to this problem, the Government announced in late 2002 that funding was being made available to provide additional prison places, including through the construction of two new prisons in Ashford and Peterborough (Home Office, 2002b).

It has frequently been observed that short (i.e. less than 12 months) custodial sentences bring little benefit either to the offender or wider society. Offenders who receive sentences of under 12 months serve half or less of the period in prison, and do not have the opportunity to undertake prison-based programmes. On release, adult offenders do not receive support or supervision from the Probation Service. Lord Woolf argued in his judgement in the burglary case of *McInerney and Keating*[6] that the shortness of these sentences was a factor which justified the greater use of community penalties. Short sentences also impose a particular logistical and administrative burden on the Prison Service. The *Review of the Sentencing Framework* (Home Office, 2001) emphasises the inadequacies of short sentences; likewise the Home Secretary has observed that:

> *Short custodial sentences provide little or no opportunity to change the behaviour and problems which put offenders there in the first place and they can have a long term adverse effect on family cohesion, on employment and on training prospects – all of which are key to the rehabilitation of offenders.* (Blunkett, 2001)

Aims of the study

The project's starting point was that the rise in imprisonment has triggered very considerable expenditure, whilst yielding few benefits in terms of crime reduction. Thus, the main aim was to look at what might discourage the use of custody by sentencers,[7] and what might encourage the use of non-custodial alternatives, thereby reversing the rise in the prison population. To this extent the study was conducted to an agenda. The study was mounted in partnership with the Prison Reform Trust (PRT). Getting the research off the ground was a collaborative enterprise, as was the dissemination of the results. However, to ensure its integrity, the research was carried out completely independently both of PRT and other bodies. It was agreed from the outset that the Trust would have no control over the content of any reports on the study. And whilst the report draws on Home Office and Prison Service statistics, and whilst government departments were kept informed of the work, the research team were in no sense accountable to them for the use we have made of these figures.

The study had five subsidiary aims:

- To explain the recent rise in the prison population;
- To identify the factors that tip a sentencing decision towards or away from the use of custody;
- To consider whether new or amended non-custodial penalties would help reduce sentencers' reliance on custody;
- To explore the impact of the social and political climate on sentencing decisions; and
- To produce recommendations on how to change sentencing practice so as to reduce the prison population.

---

6 19 December 2002.

7 The generic term used in this report for magistrates, district judges, recorders, Crown Court judges and senior judges.

The study pursued its aims through two broad lines of enquiry. It reviewed patterns and trends in adult sentencing in magistrates' courts and in the Crown Court, and it explored sentencers' decision processes – particularly in relation to cases that are on the borderline between custody and community sentences.

By combining these two levels of analysis – that is, of general sentencing practice and specific sentencing decisions – the study set out to produce a rounded view of the many and complex issues that bear on sentencing and the use of custody. The focus of this study is on the sentencing of adult offenders only. However, many of the issues explored and conclusions drawn have direct relevance also to the sentencing of young offenders.

Methods

The study involved:

- The analysis of Home Office statistics over the past decade on criminal convictions, sentencing, and the prison population;
- A review of academic and policy research on sentencing – for the most part, UK-based research;
- Focus groups with magistrates, supplemented by questionnaires distributed to participants, covering:
  - Their understanding of why the prison population has increased;
  - The social and political factors that impinge on sentencing decisions;
  - The nature of the decision-making process;
  - Their views on the range and quality of existing non-custodial penalties, and gaps in current provision; and
  - The factors that had determined whether or not to sentence offenders to custody in specific borderline cases they had dealt with.
- One-to-one, semi-structured interviews with Crown Court judges, recorders and district judges covering the same topics as the magistrates' focus groups and questionnaires;
- One-to-one, semi-structured interviews with senior judges addressing the question of why the prison population has risen and their views on sentencing practice in general.

The focus groups and interviews with sentencers were carried out in six parts of England and Wales, selected to provide a regional spread and a range of urban and rural areas:

East Midlands
Greater London
North and East
North West
South West
South Wales

Within each region, two magistrates' benches were identified – wherever possible, one being a high user and the other a low user of custody, and all with annual caseloads of over 350. Through the local justices' clerk's office, a focus group was organised with members of each bench (except in one case, in which it was not possible to arrange a group within the study's time-frame). A total of 80 magistrates took part in the 11 focus groups, and 69 questionnaires were returned by the participants. Table 1.2 provides details of the magistrates' benches involved in the focus groups.[8]

Table 1.2. Choice of magistrates' courts[(1)]

	Total proceeded against	Sentenced at the magistrates' court			Committed to Crown Court for trial (%)
		Total	Immediate custody (%)	High or low custody user	
North West A	1,653	783	18	High	8
South Wales A	1,327	538	16	High	15
North and East A	995	510	15	High	13
South West A	1,975	855	14	High	19
Greater London A	703	369	14	High	17
East Midlands A	671	372	13	High	15
North and East B	1,152	617	10	Low	13
South West B	663	365	9	Low	13

Notes (1) All indictable offences, persons aged 21 and over - 1999 figures

Figures provided by Home Office Research Development and Statistics Directorate

One-to-one interviews were held with Crown Court judges, recorders and district judges based in each of the fieldwork regions. For the most part, the sentencers were contacted through local Crown Court centres and magistrates' courts. A total of 48 interviews were held: 17 with Crown Court judges, 12 with recorders and 14 with district judges. (Among the district judges, four were also recorders, but for the purposes of analysis, these sentencers are included in the district judge category.) Additionally, five members of the senior judiciary were interviewed in London.

As noted above, the magistrates' questionnaires and the one-to-one interviews incorporated questions about how the respondents had made specific sentencing decisions. This has allowed the study insight into the key factors that tend to determine whether or not custodial sentences are passed; previous studies of sentencing have rarely focused on actual sentencing decisions, instead focusing more on hypothetical cases – exceptions being Flood-Page and Mackie (1998) and Parker, Sumner and Jarvis (1989).

Outline of the report

Chapter 2 of the report examines the statistics on sentencing and on the prison population, aiming to account for the growth in the prison population over the past 10 years. In particular, it looks at changes in custody rates and the length of prison sentences. The chapter presents a great deal of statistical material, much of which is hard for the non-specialist to grasp. It reaches the conclusion that the increase in the prison population is largely a function of sentencers' greater use of custodial sentences and their use of longer prison terms. Readers who do not need convincing of this conclusion should pass quickly to Chapter 3.

---

8 Of the eleven magistrates' benches, five were high users of imprisonment while four were low custody users. Their respective committal rates disproved the notion that there might be a simple correlation between low use of committals and high use of immediate imprisonment (and vice versa).

Chapter 3 considers the possible root causes of the changes in sentencing practice that have led to the rise in the prison population. It draws both on the existing research literature and on the views of sentencers interviewed for this study. More specifically, the chapter tests the arguments that the growth in the prison population has been brought about by greater severity on the part of sentencers and that it is a result of changes in patterns of offending.

In Chapters 4 to 6, the focus of the discussion narrows from sentencing practice in general to the specifics of how sentencers make their decisions. Chapter 4 is concerned with sentencers' accounts of their use of custody, and the ways in which they make decisions about borderline cases. In Chapter 5, sentencers' views on alternatives to custody are explored. Chapter 6 looks at sentencers' perceptions of the political and social context within which they make their decisions. Chapter 7 draws out the policy implications of this study for efforts to reverse the rise in the prison population. The major themes covered in this chapter are the legal and legislative framework of sentencing, alternatives to custody, and the climate of opinion about crime and punishment.

2 Accounting for the growth in the prison population

The focus of this report is on changes in the adult prison population.[9] The aim of this chapter is to account for the 71% rise in the adult prison population that occurred between 1991 and 2003. It examines trends in numbers of convictions, remand rates, convictions, custody rates, committal practice and release policy. Also included is an examination of changes in the use of non-custodial penalties.

The prison population

There are two factors that determine the size of the prison population. First there is the 'flow' of sentenced offenders going into prison. This is a product only of the number of offenders appearing in court, and the proportion of these who get remanded or sentenced to imprisonment. Then there is the 'stock' of prisoners – the prison population on any one day – which is a product of the flow into prison, coupled with the length of time actually served. Adults make up the vast majority of the overall prison population (84%), partly because they are more likely than young offenders to attract custodial sentences, and partly because when they do, they serve longer sentences.

Table 2.1 shows the make-up of the total sentenced prison population in 2001. The top half of the table shows receptions, or the flow of offenders into prison. Theft and motoring offences are the largest offence groups. The bottom half of the table shows the population, or the stock of offenders in prison, on 30 June 2002. Here the proportionate contribution of offences of violence, robbery and sexual offences is larger, because these categories can attract long sentences. Figures are for prisoners of all ages but they exclude those on remand.

While the vast majority of prisoners are male, the adult female prison population has grown much more rapidly over the past decade. Between 1991 and 2001 the adult male sentenced population rose from 28,606 to 42,998, an increase of 50%. Over the same period, the equivalent female population rose by 143% from 1,033 to 2,508.[10]

The proportion of black offenders in prison is far greater than in the general population (see Table 2.2). Only 2% of the general population were black in 2001; yet 13% of male prisoners were black, as were 21% of female prisoners. Whilst the over-representation has grown over the decade since 1991 for male prisoners, it has reduced for females.

---

9 'Adults' includes all those aged 21 and over.
10 Source: Prison Statistics England and Wales Table 1.9 (Home Office, 2003).

Table 2.1. Make-up of the prison population (all ages), 2001

	Violence against person	Sexual offences	Burglary	Robbery	Theft and handling	Fraud and forgery	Drug offences	Motoring offences	Other offences	Total[1]
Receptions into prison 2001										
Male	12,757	2,353	9,633	3,778	19,463	2451	6,513	14,838	9,972	81,758
%	15	3	12	5	23	3	8	18	12	100
Female	878	19	256	282	2873	537	1,009	383	857	7,094
%	12	0	4	4	40	7	14	5	12	100
Sentenced prison population 30 June 2001										
Male	11,198	5,039	8,361	6,561	4,150	893	7,936	2,630	3,678	50,446
%	22	10	17	13	8	2	16	5	7	100
Female	439	25	154	252	434	127	1,132	–	273[2]	2,836
%	15	1	5	9	15	4	40	–	10[2]	100

Notes (1) Totals exclude those held for offence not recorded and in default of payment of a fine
       (2) Includes motoring offences

Source: Prison Statistics England and Wales 2001 Tables 1.7a, 3.8 and 4.5 (Home Office, 2003).

Table 2.2. Prison[1] and general populations (all ages) of England and Wales – ethnic breakdown

Percentage (on 30 June)	White	Black	South Asian	Chinese and other
1991				
Male – prison population	84	10	3	2
Female – prison population	70	24	2	4
Male – general population	94	2	3	1
Female – general population	94	2	3	1
2001				
Male – prison population	79	13	3	4
Female – prison population	73	21	1	4
Male – general population	93	2	3	2
Female – general population	94	2	3	1

Notes (1) Figures relate to prisoners of all ages.

Source: Prison Statistics England and Wales 1991 Table 1.13 and 2001 Figure 6.2 (Home Office 1993; 2003).
General population figures are census-based, and cover all ages.

Changes in the adult prison population are shown in Table 2.3. This gives the yearly average adult prison population from 1991 to 2001, and the percentage change on 1991 figures. Figures are for all sentenced and remand prisoners. Large increases occurred from 1994 onwards, then stabilized at about 50,000 in the late 1990s, and began to rise again in 2001.

Table 2.3: Average adult (21 and over) prison population[1] [2]

Year	Average	% change on 1991	Year	Average	% change on 1991
1991[3]	36,246	–	1997	49,732	+37
1992[3]	36,775	+2	1998	53,302	+47
1993[3]	36,130	- <1	1999	52,937	+46
1994[3]	39,712	+10	2000	52,912	+46
1995[3]	41,768	+15	2001	54,376	+50
1996	44,992	+24			

Notes (1) Average adult sentenced population in custody plus average adult population on remand
(excludes all non-criminal prisoners).
(2) Includes all remand prisoners in Prison Service establishments aged 21 and over.
(3) Excludes remand prisoners in police cells (Remand prisoners were not kept in police cells from 1996 onwards).

Source: Prison Statistics England and Wales 2001, Tables 1.4 and 2.1. (Home Office 2003).

One possible factor in the increase in the prison population is a greater use of remand. The adult remand population grew by more than a third from 1991 to 1994. However, these changes predated the largest rises in the total adult prison population. The level of remand has since stabilised and in 2001 it stood at a rate lower than the 1994 figure at 8,890 (Home Office, 2003:42). These figures are shown in Table 2.4.

Table 2.4: Average population of adult (21 and over) remand prisoners in custody[1] [2]

Year	Average	% change on 1991	Year	Average	% change on 1991
1991	6,665	–	1997	9,153	+37
1992	6,824	+2	1998	9,631	+45
1993	7,943	+19	1999	9,590	+44
1994	9,235	+39	2000	8,667	+30
1995	8,517	+28	2001	8,890	+33
1996	8,672	+30			

Notes (1) All remand prisoners in Prison Service establishments aged 21 and over
(2) Excludes remand prisoners in police cells (Remand prisoners were not kept in police cells from 1996 onwards).

Source: Prison Statistics England and Wales 2001, Table 2.1 (Home Office, 2003).

From 1991 to 2001 there was a 54% increase in the average *sentenced* population (Table 2.5). This amounts to nearly 16,000 people. The average remand population increased by a third or 2,000 people over the same period. Thus while the remand population is much larger than it was a decade ago, in terms of total prison numbers, the rise in the *sentenced* prison population has had far more impact. This is why the current study focuses on decisions relating to sentencing rather than remand.

Table 2.5: Average population of adult (21 and over) sentenced prisoners in custody

Year	Average	% change on 1991	Year	Average	% change on 1991
1991	29,581	–	1997	40,579	+37
1992	29,951	+1	1998	43,671	+48
1993	28,187	-5	1999	43,347	+47
1994	30,477	+3	2000	44,245	+50
1995	33,251	+12	2001	45,486	+54
1996	36,320	+23			

Source: Prison Statistics England and Wales Table 1.4. (Home Office, 2003)

Convictions

The most obvious explanation for the increase in the sentenced prison population is that the courts are dealing with more offenders. However, this has not been the case for the last decade. Although there have been data collection problems in some areas for many years (Home Office, 2002a, appendix 2), the general trend in the number of convictions has been downward. For 1991 the recorded adult total was 1.2 million (Home Office, 1992:101). By 2001 the figure was down 11% to just under 1.1 million (Home Office, 2002a:45). Over the same period the number of adults found guilty of indictable offences fell by 1% from 220,000 to 217,400 (Home Office, 1992:100; 2002a:44).

While the number of convictions is down, it is possible that the distribution of offences has altered in such a way as to drive up the prison population. This would happen, for example, if the overall downward trend masked a rise in cases involving serious crimes. To test for this, Table 2.6 compares the offence mix of courts' workloads in 1991 and 2001.

The breakdown of convictions has not altered in a way that suggests a direct relationship to the increased use of custody. For example, the number of convictions for violence against the person,[11] sexual offences and burglary has fallen substantially. The one notable exception is a very large increase in the number of convictions for drugs offences (see also Corkery, 2002). A sizeable proportion of these will have been given custodial sentences (see below). There has also been a rise in robbery, although this offence represented just one per cent of all those found guilty for indictable offences in both 1991 and 2001.

---

11 Some of this will reflect a charging standard for assault introduced on 31 August 1994 which moved some offences to summary common assault.

Table 2.6. Adults (21 and over) found guilty at all courts – by offence group

Offence group Indictable offences	1991	2001	% change	1991 (%)	2001 (%)
Violence against the person	32,600	22,100	-32	15	10
Sexual offences	4,700	3,000	-36	2	1
Burglary	22,300	13,500	-40	10	6
Robbery	2,300	2,600	+13	1	1
Theft and handling	87,500	86,100	-2	40	40
Fraud and forgery	16,900	14,700	-13	8	7
Criminal damage	6,300	6,000	-5	3	3
Drugs offences	17,200	33,000	+92	8	15
Other offences	21,800	30,500	+40	10	14
Motoring offences	8,400	5,800	-31	4	3
Total	**220,000**	**217,400**	**-1**	**100%**	**100%**
Indictable offences	220,000	217,400	-1	18	20
Summary offences	996,600	868,300	-13	82	80
All offences	**1,216,700**	**1,085,800**	**-11**	**100%**	**100%**

Notes (1) There were shortfalls in the number of offenders found guilty in 1994, 1996, 1999, 2000 and 2001 (see Home Office, 2002a: Appendix 2).

Source: Criminal Statistics England and Wales 1991 and 2001 (Home Office, 1992, Table 5.9 and Home Office, 2002a, Table 5.7).

While the total number of those found guilty has fallen, within offence groups it is possible that changes in the seriousness of offending may have made custody more likely. There are two possibilities here. Firstly, there may have been an increase in the more serious offences within an offence *group* (e.g. more murders within 'violence against the person'). However, analysis of statistics by the Home Office has not found much evidence of this.[12] The second possibility is that serious offences within an offence *type* are now more serious (e.g. a 'typical' actual bodily harm is now more serious). This unfortunately cannot be tested by looking at the statistics, but is an issue that was explored in discussions with sentencers (see Chapter 3).

The rise in the prison population cannot be explained by greater use of remand. Similarly, it is not the result of more convictions or of changes in the broad offence breakdown of those found guilty – though the very large increase in those found guilty of drugs offences has had some impact. If these elements cannot explain the bulk of the rise in the prison population, this suggests that the key sentencing factors must be one or both of the following:

a) increased custody rate at the courts

b) increased length of sentences passed by the courts.

Some other factors may have also played a part, however – particularly changes in committal practice and in the proportion of sentences actually served, arising from changes in practice in relation to parole, automatic conditional release and other forms of early release. The chapter will return to these issues once it has considered changes in custody rates and sentence lengths.

---

12 Correspondence with Home Office Offending and Criminal Justice Group (April 2003).

Custody rates

The custody rate at court is simply the proportion of those found guilty who are given a custodial sentence. The rates recorded for adults by both magistrates' courts and the Crown Court are shown in Table 2.7.

Table 2.7. Adult (21 and over) custody rate at the courts[1]

Year	magistrates' courts %	Crown Court %	All courts %
1991	5	46	17
1996	10	61	24
1997	11	61	25
1998	13	61	25
1999	14	63	26
2000	16	64	28
2001	16	64	28

Notes (1) Persons aged 21 and over sentenced to immediate custody as a percentage of all persons of relevant age group sentenced for indictable offences.

Source: Criminal Statistics England and Wales 2001 Table 7.13 (Home Office, 2002a)

The overall adult custody rate in 2001 was approaching twice the 1991 level at 28%. Over the same period the custody rate for magistrates' courts increased more than three times from 5% to 16%. Use of custody by Crown Courts similarly rose from 46% to 64%. Table 2.8 shows how this increased reliance on imprisonment is broken down by offence group.

Table 2.8 shows that the custody rate was higher for every offence group in both types of court in 2001 than it was in 1991, excepting the very small group of women sentenced for sex offences. The change was particularly pronounced in some offence groups. The Crown Court custody rate for burglary rose from 56% to 79% and for drug offences from 55% to 73%. Theft and handling of stolen goods has made a large contribution to the growth in prison numbers because the offence group is numerically large (see Table 2.6 p11) and the custody rate has increased steeply. This rise may reflect the growth in numbers of dependent drug users who support their habit through very persistent shoplifting and other theft offences – a possibility that is explored further in Chapter 3.

Table 2.8. Adult (21 and over) custody rate at the courts by offence group – 1991 and 2001[1]

Offence group	Magistrates' courts				The Crown Court			
	1991		2001		1991		2001	
	Male %	Female %	Male %	Female %	Male %	Female %	Male %	Female %
Violence against the person[2]	5	2	19	10	47	20	61	34
Sexual offences	4	–	25	17[3]	69	43[3]	77	39[3]
Burglary	15	9	40	27	56	27	79	60
Robbery	*	*	*	*	88	60	92	79
Theft and handling	6	2	23	14	36	19	59	40
Fraud and forgery	6	2	18	9	42	23	57	34
Criminal damage	5	4	8	5	36	13	43	28
Drugs offences	2	1	4	4	55	39	73	60
Other offences	4	2	10	6	41	21	53	33
Motoring offences	2	1	10	4	49	8[3]	62	42[3]
Total indictable offences	6	2	17	11	48	23	66	45

Notes (1) Up to 1992 includes partly suspended sentences given for principal offences; the full length (i.e. the suspended and the unsuspended part) is included.
(2) A charging standard for assault was introduced in 1994 which led to increased use of the summary offence of common assault.
(3) Based on less than 100 females sentenced.

Source: Criminal Statistics England and Wales Tables 7.15 and 7.16 (Home Office, 2002a).

Breaking down the broad offence groups into narrower categories, more specific patterns emerged. Using figures for all offenders, irrespective of age, there have been the following increases in custody rates:

	1991	2001
Burglary in a dwelling:	37%	60%
Burglary not in a dwelling:	21%	37%
Wounding Section 20 – Grievous Bodily Harm:	28%	54%
Wounding Section 47- Actual Bodily Harm:	10%	27%
Driving whilst disqualified (magistrates' courts):	18%	47%

(Figures provided by Home Office RDS)

Sentence length

As discussed above, the 'flow' of sentenced offenders going into prison is a product only of the number of offenders appearing in court, and the proportion of these who get remanded or imprisoned. The 'stock' of prisoners – the prison population on any one day – is a product of the flow into prison, coupled with the length of time actually served. Sentence length is a key determinant of the size of the prison population.

However, identifying trends in sentence length is not straightforward. The rapid rise in the proportion of offenders sent to prison means that those who previously might have been given a community penalty are now serving short prison sentences, typically for six months or less. This has the effect of masking any increases in other sentence length categories. The average length of adult sentences fell between 1991 and 2001 (Home Office, 2003:93). In 1991 the average length was 19 months. By 1994 this had fallen to 15.7 and by 2001 it was

15.4 months.[13] In order to identify trends within different sentence length categories Figure 2.1 puts adult sentences into three groups by length.

Figure 2.1. Receptions into prison: adults (21 and over) under sentence by sentence length – indexed to 1991 figures

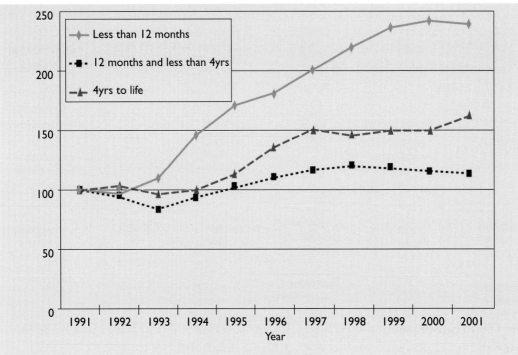

Source: Prison Statistics England and Wales 2001, Table 1.12 (Home Office, 2003)

The number of receptions has increased over the past decade for all three sentence length groups. As expected, the rise in prisoners with short sentences is by far the steepest, showing an increase of 139%, from just over 19,000 adults in 1991 to over 46,000 in 2001. Over the same period, those with sentences of 12 months to less than four years increased by 13% from over 15,000 to just over 17,000, while those with four years to life rose by 62% from nearly 4,000 to over 6,000 (see Home Office, 2003:28).

It would be a misreading of Figure 2.1 to suggest that the rise in the prison population can be attributed largely to increases in short sentences. Even if the number of short sentence prisoners increased quickly, they may make a smaller contribution to the total prison population than those serving long sentences. A typical lifer will occupy a prison cell for the same amount of time as a hundred short sentence offenders sentenced in magistrates courts.[14] Thus the rise of 62% in sentences of four years or more will have had a very significant impact on the overall population.

Long sentences are almost certainly getting even longer. As discussed above, the difficulty in identifying the trend is that changes in the custody rate tend to increase the proportion of short-sentence prisoners. There has certainly been greater use of life sentences from 1995 onwards (Home Office, 2003:100). By 2001 the number of adults in prison under life sentence was 67% higher than in 1991, an increase from 2,750 to over 4,500.[15] The best way of examining trends in sentence length is to look within offence groups, where one can assume a degree of homogeneity over time, at the breakdown of sentence length (Table 2.9).

13 Figures exclude those sentenced to life imprisonment.

14 Assuming that the lifer serves about 13 years, and that the average sentence in magistrates courts is about three months.

15 Population at June 30. (Prison Statistics England and Wales, 2001, Table 5.1 – Home Office, 2003:100). The increase in the late 1990s has been influenced by the Crime (Sentences) Act 1997 which stipulates an automatic life sentence for a second serious violent or sexual assault.

Table 2.9 needs careful interpretation. The offence groups where short sentences have become proportionately more significant are ones where the courts have become more likely to impose custodial rather than community penalties. For example, the growth of short sentences for theft and handling will reflect the fact that offenders who previously would have been given fines or community penalties are now getting prison sentences. This offence group did [...] long sentences in either 1991 or 2001.

[...] e groups that show no real change, such as violence against the person, the [...] te has probably interacted with an increase in average sentence length, to [...] erall change. In other words, the courts are passing short sentences on a [...] f offenders for minor assaults – depressing average sentence lengths – whilst [...] the prison terms awarded for more serious violence – increasing average

[...] e clearly become longer in cases of rape and other sexual offences. The [...] iddle-range sentences has shrunk while the proportion getting long [...] There is a similar pattern for burglary, except that the shift has been [...] to middle-range ones, while in others there has been a shift in the [...] a rise in life sentences given for robbery, though short sentences have [...] tainly reflecting a rise in the custody rate. When all offence types are [...] ncrease has been in long sentences at the expense of middle-range

[...] al changes in use of long or short sentences in terms of [...] 21 and over) – 30 June 1991 to 30 June 2001 [1] [2]

	Rape	Other sexual offences	Burglary	Robbery	Theft and forgery	Drugs offences	Other offences	Offences not recorded	Total
	–	–	–	+1	+7	–	+14	-2	+2
	–	–	-1	–	+9	-1	+5	–	+1
	–	–	-5	–	+1	-2	-5	–	-3
	–	-1	-9	–	-7	-2	-2	+1	-4
	-3	-1	-1	–	-7	+2	-6	+1	-3
	-4	–	+10	+4	-1	+7	-1	+2	+3
	-8	–	+5	+3	–	+2	-2	-1	+2
	+1	+2	+1	-8	-2	-8	-4	-2	–
	-8	+2	-1	-2	–	+2	–	-1	+1
	6	–	–	+2	–	–	–	+1	+1
	Longer	Longer	Generally shorter	Shorter		No overall change	Shorter	No overall change	Generally longer

[...] or shorter, positive changes are in bold.

[...] an 1%.

[...] 1991 Tables 4.1 and 5.1; 2001 Table 4.1 (Home Office, 1993; 2003)

Sentence length by type of court

Figure 2.2 shows how the length of sentence imposed at each venue has altered over time for male offenders guilty of indictable offences. The average length of custodial sentence given by magistrates' courts showed an increase in the early 1990s, especially for 1993 and 1994. In terms of sentence length this may not appear to be a large change (from 2.6 months, for adult male offenders in 1991, to 3.2 months in 1993). However, the high volume of cases that magistrates deal with may mean that this would have had a significant impact on the total prison population. By 1997 the average male sentence length given by magistrates' courts was back down to 1991 levels, and even fell slightly below this for 2000 and 2001. While magistrates' courts were sending more people to prison, the length of sentence was in fact slightly lower in 2001 than it was 10 years before.

Figure 2.2. Average length of sentence given by the Crown Court and by magistrates' courts for all adult males (21 and over) – all indictable offences

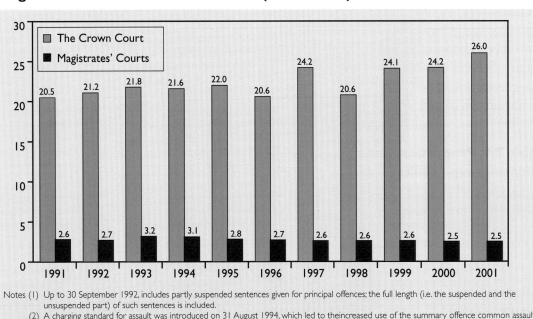

Notes (1) Up to 30 September 1992, includes partly suspended sentences given for principal offences; the full length (i.e. the suspended and the unsuspended part) of such sentences is included.
(2) A charging standard for assault was introduced on 31 August 1994, which led to the increased use of the summary offence common assault.
(3) Excludes life sentences.

Source: Criminal Statistics England and Wales 2001, Tables 7.15 and 7.16 (Home Office 2002).

The average length of custodial sentence given by the Crown Court has generally been increasing across the whole period, but especially from 1995 to 2001. The average sentence given to adult males has increased by a third from 20.5 months in 1991 to 26 months in 2001. Such a large increase in Crown Court sentence length will have been a major factor in increasing the prison population.

Changes in procedure

While the main causes behind the rise in the prison population are identified as changes in the two types of courts' custody rates and in sentence length, other factors have also had some impact. Important changes relate to committal procedure, and to the way in which practice relating to parole and automatic release have affected the proportion of sentences served in prison.

Committal practice

The Crown Court deals with a much smaller number of cases than magistrates' courts, but these are the more serious ones, where use of custody is frequent. Figure 2.2 showed that the Crown Court has been giving increasingly longer sentences. Earlier research has also shown that the Crown Court imposes heavier sentences than magistrates' courts, even when they are hearing equivalent cases (Hedderman and Moxon, 1992). Thus, a shift in the number or type of cases dealt with at either venue could affect the prison population. Figure 2.3 shows how committal procedure has changed between 1991 and 2001.

Between 1991 and 1997 the number of defendants appearing at the Crown Court for trial ranged from 66,000 to 75,000 and followed no particular pattern. The same can be said for those committed for sentence after summary conviction, which ranged from 2,600 to 5,000. However, the situation changed in 1998 resulting in fewer defendants appearing for trial, but a threefold increase in those being sent from magistrates' courts for sentence (see Figure 2.3). This was a response to the *plea before venue* procedure introduced on 1 October 1997.[16] Previously, magistrates had to decide on mode of trial without knowing how a defendant intended to plead. From October 1997 defendants charged with offences triable either way had to indicate a plea *before* the mode of trial decision was taken (Home Office, 1997). The result was an increase in the number of defendants committed to the Crown Court for sentence (see also Ayres *and colleagues*, 2000).

Figure 2.3. Adult defendants (21 and over) committed to trial or sentence at Crown Court

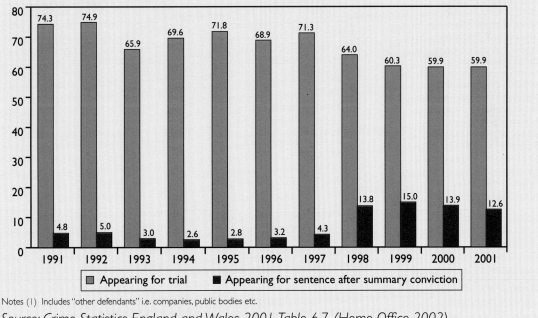

Notes (1) Includes "other defendants" i.e. companies, public bodies etc.

Source: Crime Statistics England and Wales 2001, Table 6.7. (Home Office 2002).

---

16 Section 49 of the Criminal Procedure and Investigations Act 1996 (with provisions for committal for sentence contained in section 51 of the Crime (Sentences) Act 1997), Home Office (1997).

The total number of adult defendants at the Crown Court was actually less in 2001 than in 1991, falling from 79,100 to 72,500. However, it is not the workload that is of interest so much as the numbers being convicted at each venue. Although the number of adults convicted of indictable offences has remained fairly stable (see Table 2.6 above), the number appearing at the Crown Court for sentence has increased. This is likely to have resulted in the imposition of heavier sentences for these individuals than if they had stayed within the magistrates' court.

The make-up of the prison population in terms of the sentencing venue is shown in Figure 2.4.

Figure 2.4. Adult population (21 and over) in prison by sentencing

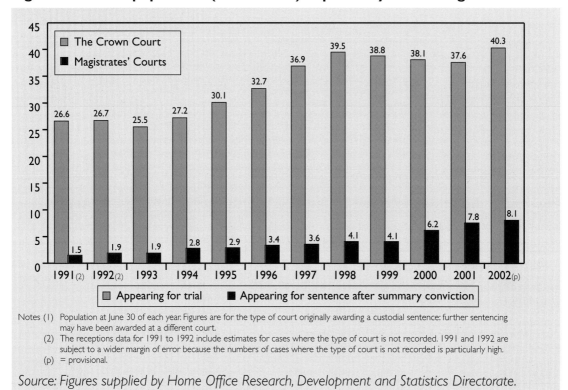

Notes (1)   Population at June 30 of each year. Figures are for the type of court originally awarding a custodial sentence: further sentencing may have been awarded at a different court.
      (2)   The receptions data for 1991 to 1992 include estimates for cases where the type of court is not recorded. 1991 and 1992 are subject to a wider margin of error because the numbers of cases where the type of court is not recorded is particularly high.
      (p)   = provisional.

Source: Figures supplied by Home Office Research, Development and Statistics Directorate.

While both magistrates' courts and the Crown Court have been sending more people to custody, it is clear from Figure 2.4 that during the 1990s the rise in the prison population was largely down to Crown Court decisions. From 2000 to 2001 there has been a fall in prisoner numbers resulting from Crown Court decisions, and a rise resulting from magistrates' courts decisions.

Release policy and practice

Decisions affecting prisoners' release dates can obviously affect the size of the prison population. Table 2.10 compares the proportion of time served in 1991 and in 2001, for adult males. It shows that the proportion of time served has decreased for shorter sentences, but increased for longer sentences. The effect of the change for longer sentences will have inflated prison numbers much more than the change for shorter sentences will have deflated them.

Table 2.10. Average length of sentence, in months[1] – all adult males (21 and over) 1991 and 2001

Adult males	1991		2001	
	average length of sentence	Percentage of sentence served under sentence	average length of sentence	Percentage of sentence served under sentence
Up to and including 3 mths	2	42	2.1	39
> 3 mths to 6 mths	5.3	43	4.8	39
> 6 mths but < 12 mths	10.2	41	8.7	37
12 mths			12	38
> 12 mths to 18 mths	16.6	42	16.4	41
> 18 mths to 3 yrs	28	42	28.3	43
> 3 yrs but < 4 yrs	45.7	49	42.3	43
4 yrs			48	54
> 4 yrs to 5 yrs	58.1	49	57.5	55
> 5 yrs to 10 yrs	84.6	53	85.4	53
> 10 yrs but < life	177.2	49	158.2	55
All lengths of sentence less than life	**18.4**	**46**	**16.3**	**46**

Notes (1) Excludes time served on remand.

Source: Prison Statistics England and Wales 1991 Table 4.15; 2001 Table 4.11 (Home Office, 1993; 2003).

Changes in release policy have contributed to this shift. Firstly, a decision by the Carlisle Review Committee (Carlisle, 1988) led to a risk-based release policy for parole which was then incorporated into the Criminal Justice Act 1991.[17] As Hood and Shute (2000:4) have noted, the Carlisle Committee had hoped that this would cause more long-term prisoners to be released earlier. However, by 1993 the Parole Board recognised that this would actually lead to a lower paroling rate (Parole Board, 1994:para 138).[18]

The Criminal Justice Act 1991 brought about further changes in parole which could have led to longer time served. The most notable change was in the timing of parole eligibility and eligibility for conditional release. Prisoners serving four years or more became eligible for parole at half their sentence, rather than at a third as before (Discretionary Conditional Release). For those serving less than four years, Automatic Conditional Release was introduced at half the sentence (rather than possible parole at a third), to be followed by probation supervision until three-quarters. Coinciding with the implementation of the Act in October 1992, Lord Chief Justice Taylor issued a Practice Statement[19] which acknowledged that "…sentences on the 'old' scale would under the 'new' Act result in many prisoners actually serving longer in custody than hitherto". He recommended "a new approach" with Crown Court sentencers taking the "actual period likely to be served" into account and taking into account the risk of increasing sentence length following the Act. However, despite this, the average length of sentence given by the Crown Court continued to rise from 1992[20] (see Figure 2.2 above), suggesting no generalised impact from the Practice Statement (Henham, 1996).

17 This came into force 1 October 1992.

18 Quoted in Hood and Shute (2000:4).

19 Practice Statement (Crime: Sentencing) [1992] 1 WLR

20 Despite a slight dip in 1994, the average length of Crown Court sentences continued to rise through to 1997.

The situation has more recently been further complicated by the introduction of Home Detention Curfews on 28 January 1999. With a few exceptions, most prisoners in England and Wales aged 18 or over, serving sentences of less than four years – but more than three months – became eligible for early release on curfew for up to 60 days (Dodgson, Mortimer and Sugg, 2000). This had the effect of reducing the proportion of time served for shorter sentences.

The use of non-custodial penalties

Over the last ten years there has been a large increase in the use of community penalties. Table 2.11 compares figures for 2001 with 1991. Much effort has been invested over the decade in improving the quality of provision and the rigour of enforcement of community orders. As will be discussed in Chapter 4, sentencers have largely welcomed this. However, Table 2.11 shows how this has been at the expense of fines, rather than of custody. From 1991 to 2001, the use of community orders rose by over half, but the use of fines fell by nearly a third.[21]

Table 2.11. Use of community penalties – Adults (21 and over) 1991 and 2001

	Fine	CRO	CPO	CPRO	Curfew Order	DTTO	Total (excl. fines)
Male							
1991	73,600	15,800	14,700	-	-	-	30,500
2001	49,500	22,400	16,000	4,100	800	2,900	46,200
% change	-33	+42	+9	n.a.[(1)]	n.a.[(2)]	n.a.[(3)]	+51
Female							
1991	8,300	5,000	1,200	-	-	-	6,200
2001	6,800	7,100	2,600	700	100	500	11,000
% change	-18	+42	+117	n.a.[(1)]	n.a.[(2)]	n.a.[(3)]	+77
Total							
1991	81,900	20,800	15,900	-	-	-	36,700
2001	56,300	29,500	18,600	4,800	900	3,400	57,200
% change	-31	+42	+17	n.a.[(1)]	n.a.[(2)]	n.a.[(3)]	+56

Notes (1) CPROs (or combination orders as they were then termed) were introduced in 1992.
       (2) Curfew Orders were introduced in 1996.
       (3) DTTOs were introduced fully in 2000.

Source: Criminal Statistics England and Wales 2001 Table 7.10 (Home Office, 2002a).

The decline in the use of fines has indirect but important consequences for the prison population. If offenders now receive community penalties earlier in their criminal careers than 10 years ago, they will exhaust the alternatives to imprisonment more rapidly than previously. The proportion of offenders given community penalties that have no previous convictions has steadily risen over the last decade. For example, in 1991 11% of those given CROs had no previous convictions. By 2001 this figure was 27%. For those given CPOs, the figure has risen from 14% to 51% (Home Office, 2002c:25). It has been argued, for example by Morgan (2003), that a large number of such lower risk offenders could, and should, be dealt with through fines. Sentencers' shift from the use of fines to community penalties will have strained the resources of the probation service, arguably increasing the risk of failure for offenders given community penalties. However, demonstrating this is hard, given that at the same time

---

21 While there has been less use of fines, there has also been a fall in the use of custody for fine defaulters.

there was a marked 'toughening up' in the way that the probation service policed offenders' compliance with the conditions of their orders.

Summary

The factors that have driven up the prison population are complex and interwoven. But the key factors are simple to grasp. The courts are more likely to use custodial sentences now than a decade ago, and when they do, they are more likely to pass longer sentences. No more offenders are appearing before the courts than ten years ago, so this cannot explain the growth in the prison population.

Increased custody rates

- The Crown Court and magistrates' courts have increased their custody rates across all offence groups.

- The overall adult custody rate in 2001 was approaching twice the 1991 level. Over the same period the custody rate for magistrates' courts increased more than three times from 5% to 16%. Use of custody by Crown Courts similarly rose from 46% to 64%.

- Increased use of imprisonment for the numerically large group of offences involving theft and handling of stolen goods has had an impact on the prison population.

Increased length of sentences

- There has been a numerical increase in very short sentences, but these are at the expense of community penalties or fines, rather than middle-length prison sentences.

- As magistrates' courts have been sending more people to prison, the average length of sentence given was in fact slightly lower in 2001 than it was ten years before.

- However, sentence lengths in the Crown Court have been increasing.

- There has also been greater use of longer sentences at the expense of middle-range sentences.

- Lengthier sentences are particularly evident for sexual offences and burglary.

Other factors

- The rise in the prison population cannot be explained by greater use of remand.

- There has been a substantial rise in numbers found guilty of drugs offences. This will have affected the prison population, as offences of supply typically attract custody.

- Other procedural changes have played a part in pushing up the prison population. The main factors here are changes in committal practice and changes in parole or automatic release.

- There has been a decline in the use of fines which has had indirect consequences for the prison population – if offenders are given community penalties earlier in their criminal careers, they will exhaust the alternatives to imprisonment more rapidly than in the past.

3 Understanding the growth in the prison population

Chapter 2 identified two main reasons why the prison population has risen over the last decade: sentencers are sending a higher proportion of offenders to prison, and medium to long prison sentences have got longer. This chapter examines what factors underlie these sentencing trends. There are two main possible explanations.

The first is simply that sentencers have become more severe in their sentencing decisions. Comparing like with like, they may be more likely to pass prison sentences now than a decade ago, and when they do, they may be more likely to pass long sentences than previously. There are several reasons why this might have happened, not least a less tolerant climate of political and public opinion about crime and punishment, to which sentencers have responded. The second possible explanation is that offenders appearing before the courts now have longer records or have committed more serious crimes than those under sentence 10 years ago. It was noted in Chapter 2 that there have been no gross changes either in the volume or in the 'offence-mix' of sentencers' workloads.[22] It remains possible, however, that assaults or robberies or burglaries committed now have more aggravating features – associated with the offence or the offender – than those in the early 1990s. There are good reasons for thinking that this may have happened, notably the growth in the population of drug dependent persistent offenders.

It has proved hard to test these hypotheses definitively or exhaustively. Assessing if sentencing has become more severe requires answers to hypothetical questions about the way sentencers would have treated the same cases had they heard them 10 years earlier. Some evidence can be brought to bear, but as often as not, it is circumstantial. Questions about changes in persistence are also hard to answer, as will emerge, because of the complexity and relative inaccessibility of the databases needed to test out the possibilities. And some of the arguments put by many respondents that 'crime has got nastier' are often not amenable to statistical measurement.

Has sentencing become more severe?

It is an orthodoxy amongst penal commentators, those involved in penal policy and – as observed below – the senior judiciary, that sentencers have got tougher, and that this shift is in large measure a response to the climate of opinion about crime and punishment.[23] And indeed there is plenty of circumstantial evidence to this effect.

In October 1992 the Government implemented key provisions of the 1991 Criminal Justice Act, a piece of legislation whose guiding principle was parsimony in the use of imprisonment for non-violent offenders. Over the following three months the prison population began to fall, as indeed was the legislative intention. However the New Year of 1993 saw several brutal murders, most notably that of two-year-old James Bulger. The press, led by the Daily Mail, made excoriating attacks on the reforms introduced by the 1991 Act, painting a picture of liberal do-gooders wrecking the criminal justice system whilst crime spiralled out of control. The prison population began to rise almost immediately.

---

22 Though some 'prison-prone' offence groups have risen, notably those involving offences of drug supply.

23 See Ashworth and Hough (1996) for an early formulation of this view. See also Dunbar and Langdon (1998), Hedderman (2003) and Morgan (2003).

In the face of mounting criticism the Government was quick to abandon its decarceral policy, amending the Criminal Justice Act to remove some of the new restrictions on sentencers' powers to pass prison sentences.[24] The amendments actually took effect in August 1993, but sentencers appear to have anticipated the legislation well before this. By October 1994 the Government had rid itself of all trace of its decarceral policies. The then Home Secretary, Michael Howard, announced a set of 27 'get tough' policies under the banner 'Prison Works'. There was little challenge from New Labour, then in opposition, which had positioned itself as 'tough on crime, tough on the causes of crime'. Thereafter the prison population continued to rise.

The legislative and legal framework

Many changes in sentencing practice come about as a direct result of changes to the legislative and legal framework. The maximum sentences for offences are set out in statute; and whilst judges rarely pass sentences approaching the maximum, changes to the legislation are taken as an indication of the intentions of the legislature in calling for heavier (or lighter) penalties. Increasingly, legislation is also tending to set out mandatory minimum sentences in specified circumstances. Guideline judgements issued by the Court of Appeal provide another mechanism for shaping and containing sentencers' discretion. Finally, the Magistrates Association has since the mid-1990s issued several versions of a manual setting out sentencing guidelines for use in magistrates' courts.

Leaving aside the 1991 and 1993 Criminal Justice Acts, the key relevant legislative changes over the period covered by this study are:

- The extension of prosecutorial appeals against sentence to certain either-way offences in 1994 (following their introduction for indictable only offences in 1988)

- The introduction of the offence of aggravated vehicle taking in 1992, with tougher penalties for 'joyriding'

- The doubling of the maximum sentence for causing death by dangerous driving and related offences in the Criminal Justice Act 1993

- The mandatory minimum prison terms introduced by the Crime (Sentences) Act 1997, and implemented in 1999, for third-time drug traffickers and burglars

- The introduction of automatic life sentences for a second serious violent or sexual assault following the Crime (Sentences) Act 1997

- The introduction of racially aggravated offences in the Crime and Disorder Act 1998

- The raising of the maximum sentence for incitement of racial hatred from 2 years to 7 years.

Most of these changes were targeted on specific offence categories, some of which are numerically small. Moreover, the provisions for mandatory minimum sentences were targeted at those with relevant previous convictions – an even smaller sub-group of offenders. The overall impact on the prison population might thus be thought to be limited. However the changes are very likely to have had knock-on effects on other types of crime. The more that sentencers aim to achieve proportionality in their sentencing – with offences of similar gravity and culpability receiving similar sentences – the more marked these knock-on effects will be (cf Woolf, 2002). It is also significant that all these legislative changes have created pressure in the same upward direction on the prison population.

---

24 The amendments in the 1993 Criminal Justice Act did little more than clarify the law about 'sentencing on record', reverting to the position prior to the 1991 Act; but they had a symbolic importance in signaling a move away from the philosophy of the 1991 Act.

There were also some significant guideline judgements in the 1990s and the establishment of the Sentencing Advisory Panel in 1999 generated further guideline judgements. Significant ones related to causing death by dangerous driving (in support of the legislative change) and to rape. Prominent recent guidelines include those laid down by the Lord Chief Justice in January 2002 relating to the use of custody for mobile phone robberies.[25] Judgements covering many other types of crime were also made. As has been observed by Dunbar and Langdon, it is generally believed that the Court of Appeal – because of the nature of its workload and the previous experiences of its judges – "operates the highest tariff of all and … takes a view of less serious offences that is markedly more severe than the view of the lower courts" (1998: 69).

Precisely how responsive judges are to guideline judgements is unclear, but they were evidently significant in the eyes of some of the Crown Court respondents in this study; and a few of the sentencers talked in terms of proofing their decisions against prosecutorial appeals against sentence. It was suggested that guideline judgements, in combination with the possibility of prosecutorial appeal, served to draw lenient judges' decisions up to the guideline level, whilst leaving those of tougher judges unchanged. And as with legislative change, one would expect guideline judgements for specific crime types to have a knock-on effect on other crimes, given the priority placed by sentencers on achieving parity and proportionality.[26] This is likely to happen whether the guideline judgement in question is concerned with the decision to imprison or the decision about sentence length.

Of course not all guideline judgements will push up the prison population. Influential judgements by the Court of Appeal in *Ollerenshaw* (in 1999) and, more recently, *Mills* and *Kefford* (both 2002) encouraged judges to use prison sentences sparingly and with reference to prison capacity.[27] In June 2002, the Home Secretary and Lord Chancellor issued a joint statement in which they "welcomed guidance from the Lord Chief Justice" which stressed the importance of keeping prison as a last resort, and "stressed the suitability of alternatives to custody in many cases".[28] In the course of the fieldwork conducted for this study there was the further case of *McInerney and Keating*[29] relating to house burglars who would previously have received a sentence of 18 months or less. In these instances, the judgement stated that "A custodial sentence should only be resorted to if the offender had demonstrated by his behaviour that punishment in the community was not practicable." This has widely been regarded as referring to first time offenders. As noted by Davies and Tyner (2003), the case "provoked unusual levels of media criticism and public debate".[30]

Court of Appeal guideline judgements generally have limited relevance for magistrates, and for this reason the Magistrates Association has developed its own sentencing guidelines. These were first introduced in the 1970s for motoring offences, but in 1989 were extended to cover most offences dealt with by magistrates. The guidelines have since been further developed and reissued. Some of the magistrates in the study argued that these guidelines had had an inflationary effect on the prison population. This was partly because some of the 'entry points' – or recommended sentences for typical cases – were higher in the guidelines than in previous practice, or were adjusted upwards as new versions of the guidelines were issued. For example, the starting point for actual bodily harm assaults was raised from community service in the 1993 version of the guidelines to a short custodial sentence in the 1997 guidelines. It is also likely that, as with Court of Appeal guideline judgements, the Magistrates'

---

25 Attorney-General's Reference Nos. 4 and 7 of 2002, and Q [2002] 2 Cr App R (SS) 77. The Youth Justice Board Annual Review of 2001/2 notes that there was a significant rise in numbers of young offenders in custody following the Lord Chief Justice's judgement on mobile phone robberies.

26 The principle of parity means that guideline judgements about sentence length will have an impact on the custody threshold, and judgements about the custody threshold will have an impact on sentence length.

27 *Ollerenshaw* [1999] 1 Cr App R (S) 65; *Kefford* [2002] 2 Cr App R (S) 495; *Mills* (unreported 14 January 2002).

28 LCD Press Notices 194/02.

29 19 December 2002

30 In response to criticisms of the judgement, the Lord Chancellor appeared on the Today programme on Radio 4 (6 January 2003) to defend it; and on 14 January Lord Woolf issued a clarifying statement, which asserted that the guideline 'was doing no more than changing the emphasis' in the sentencing of domestic burglars (LCD Press Notices 10/03).

Association guidelines draw lenient sentencers up to the recommended norm, whilst leaving the decisions of tougher sentencers untouched.

One would expect to see a complex interplay between the climate of opinion about crime and punishment, the political and legislative response to this climate and the judicial reaction to both the climate of opinion and legislative change. The climate of opinion both shapes, and is shaped by, political responses to crime. It would be troubling if the judiciary showed no response to the climate of opinion, and very troubling if it showed no response to legislative change. On the other hand, over-responsiveness to the climate of opinion is equally undesirable. Figure 3.1 charts the rise of the prison population against key events from January 1990 until July 2002. Although it leaves room for argument, it offers some circumstantial evidence of responsiveness amongst sentencers to both legislative change and to the climate of opinion about crime and punishment.

Figure 3.1 The rise in the prison population: key events and policy interventions.

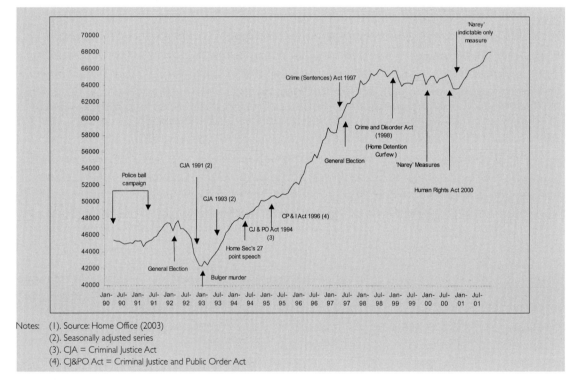

Notes: (1). Source: Home Office (2003)
          (2). Seasonally adjusted series
          (3). CJA = Criminal Justice Act
          (4). CJ&PO Act = Criminal Justice and Public Order Act

Respondents' views about sentencing severity

The sentencers who took part in this study had mixed views as to whether the rise in the prison population reflected increased severity of sentencing. The senior judges were unanimous in thinking that sentencing has become more severe over the last decade, and that this was a central factor in explaining the rise in the prison population. One, for example, commented that the rise in the prison population had been caused by 'external pressure': that is, the public's desire to see people punished. Another said a punitive political culture has been a factor:

> *Undoubtedly all the drivers from all the political parties have been for longer and longer sentences, and that feeds through. The climate is punitive.* [senior judge]

It was also suggested that judges, at least in part, are responding to pressures from the mass media for tougher punishment. These views echo those expressed by Lord Bingham, the then Lord Chief Justice, in 1998:

> *Since 1993 the use of custody has increased very sharply, in response (it would seem likely) to certain highly publicised cases, legislation, ministerial speeches and intense media pressure.*[31]

Eleven out of 15 Crown Court judges interviewed[32] pointed to greater severity of sentencing as a factor in the growth of the prison population. However, only three of the eleven seemed to view this as the primary factor, and the majority referred to tougher sentencing for particular categories of crime such as causing death by dangerous driving or sexual offences. One referred to society having become 'too punitive', and said that magistrates in particular were making greater use of custody; another said that the Crown Court is now tougher on a range of offences including sex and drugs offences. Others among the Crown Court judges spoke of there being some toughening up of sentencing (without differentiating between the magistrates' and Crown Court), but cited this as a supplementary rather than a major cause of the rising prison population.

Seven of the judges mentioned that over recent years there had been public or political pressures for greater severity in sentencing. For example, one noted that there is a public 'clamour' for custody in relation to street crime. Another commented that sentencing practice has firmed up in response to the efforts by each successive government to demonstrate that it is tougher on crime than those that went before. And a third said that judges may be less lenient than in the past because of fears of criticism in the press:

> *I think that there's much more attention in the press to the sentences that are passed. And whereas in the past, perhaps, people might have taken a very lenient course, it may be that fear of attracting extremely bad publicity for taking a lenient course means that sentences that pander to that, to a certain extent, are passed.* [Crown Court judge]

Among the recorders there was a similar mix of views on the extent to which increasing punitiveness has contributed to the growth of the prison population. Three of the 12 recorders interviewed were outspoken in their opinion that the toughening up of sentencing is the primary factor; while a further four cited this as one among other factors. One recorder commented that there has been a major change in sentencing practice, reflecting a shift towards emphasising the individual responsibility of offenders:

> *There was unquestionably a huge cultural shift. I sensed it – in the early 1980s people still talked very much in terms of an offender's personal problems, social pressures. Then there was an emphasis on individual responsibility – a focus on the individual rather than society. Therefore those charged with offences were seen as more responsible for them.* [recorder]

He also argued that the 'colossal sentences' now imposed on drugs offenders have had an impact on the prison population. Another of the recorders argued that wave after wave of legislation has had the effect of driving judges towards prison sentences, because this was what was wanted by successive Home Secretaries striving to be seen as 'tough on crime'. Others also referred to the impact on sentencing of more punitive legislation; and two argued that the way in which judicial training is organised may have the effect of encouraging the use of custody. For example:

---

31 *Brewster* [1998] 1 Cr App R (S) 181, at p. 184.

32 Although a total of 17 Crown Court judges were interviewed for this study, views on the causes of the rise in the prison population were elicited from only 15 of them.

> *I wonder if the effect [of training] has been to firm up judges who might otherwise be softer or a bit more inventive about sentencing. My guess is as soon as you're more systematic about it, you end up with more custodial sentences – probably because the environment at JSB courses tends to be quite weighted towards custodial sentencing exercises – and that becomes an internalised norm.* [recorder]

District judges and magistrates were less inclined than the other sentencers to talk about sentencing practice becoming more severe. Indeed, only two of the 14 district judges interviewed referred to this. One of these two noted that politicians have raised public expectations for tougher treatment of offenders, and that the courts have responded to this. The other said that magistrates' courts might be treating drink driving offences more severely, and that the Crown Court is imposing longer custodial sentences for certain offences.

In most of the magistrates' focus groups there was general and firm agreement that there has been little or no change in sentencing practice by magistrates in recent years. Only one of the groups argued that their bench has used custody significantly more over recent years in response to pressure from the centre to do so. One of the participants in this group said that they had become 'tougher' through adhering to the Magistrates Association guidelines:

> *... because of the guidelines, and the sentencing structure yes, because we set out on a path when we come out into the retiring room. And as we're going back, going over again about the sentencing guidelines, and we're there, and nothing can move us out of that custody box. We're there and therefore, you know, maybe four years, five years ago we'd have been, oh 'iffy', ... but now ...*

In two of the other focus groups there was some suggestion that there had been a toughening up of sentencing practice among magistrates: this was related to the impact of liaison judge training in the one case, and to the use of sentencing guidelines in the other. Some of the magistrates, while insisting that sentencing practice among magistrates had remained constant, pointed to changes elsewhere: in three groups it was argued that the severity of district judges had contributed to the prison population, and in another the severity of the Crown Court was mentioned.

Has offending increased in seriousness?

Previous research and statistics have done little to explore the competing explanation for the rise in the prison population – that sentencers are making greater use of prison because the offenders who come before the courts are there for more serious offences. As was discussed in Chapter 2, there has been no gross shift in the 'offence mix' of cases coming before the courts. However, it is possible that the figures mask some changes in offending behaviour that have had an impact on sentencing. These changes may be of two main kinds:

- offenders may be more prolific, accumulating longer criminal histories;
- offences within offence categories may be more serious.

The research team inevitably brought its own preconceptions about crime trends to this study, including the belief that the *quality* of offending was unlikely to have changed much over a decade. However, as will be discussed in more detail below, several respondents argued that they were seeing more prolific offenders – echoing the argument made by Lord Woolf (2001) that more prolific offending is a primary cause of the increased prison population. Several also advanced the argument that the crimes of offenders appearing before them had become much 'nastier'. Both propositions were often linked to the rising prevalence of drug and alcohol misuse.

Prolific offending

Published statistics suggest that there has been no growth in the proportion of persistent offenders appearing before the courts. In fact the proportion of court appearances for males where the offender had no previous convictions (for standard list offences) grew from 27% in 1993 to 42% in 2000[33] – a trend partly accounted for by reductions in the use of police cautions. The proportion of appearances for males where the offenders had ten or more previous court appearances has fallen from 19% to 17%; the figure for female offenders was 7% in both years. However the figures raise as many questions as they answer. Why should there have been such a large increase in first offenders? Are a third of burglary appearances really for first offences?

It is possible that a more fine-grained analysis that identified the proportion of offenders with 20 or 30 previous court appearances might shed more light on the issue of whether there is greater persistence of offending within some crime categories. For the time being, it seems that the available evidence is too inconclusive either to rule out or to confirm the hypothesis.

In one crime category – theft and handling of stolen goods – there is some evidence of a growth in persistence: 21% of male appearances were for offenders with 10 or more previous appearances in 1993, a figure that rose to 26% in 2000. The equivalent figure for female appearances were 7% and 12%. As noted in Chapter 2, the custody rate for this offence group has increased sharply. However, the relationship between prolific offending and use of custody for theft and handling is not straightforward, since the increase in the custody rate appears to be disproportionate to the increase in persistence of offending.

While the published statistics on offenders do not provide definitive answers about the persistence of offending, there is some plausibility to sentencers' claims that they are seeing more offenders with long criminal records before the courts. This is because of the growth in dependent drug use, and the relationship between dependent drug use and offending. Recent research suggests the number of dependent drug users has increased very rapidly over the last 10 years,[34] and that there could now be upward of a quarter of a million problem drug users in Britain today (Godfrey *et al.*, 2002; Audit Commission, 2002). The links between dependent drug use and offending are strong – if complex (see Hough, 1996; Hough *et al.*, 2002). Large proportions of arrestees test positive for heroin or cocaine at the time of arrest (Bennett *et al.*, 2001; MHA Matrix and Nacro, 2003).[35] The increase in persistence of those convicted for theft and handling is consistent with the hypothesis that there is a growing number of drug dependent persistent offenders – as shoplifting, their preferred fund-raising strategy, is the biggest single crime category in this group of offences.

If it is correct that offending has become more prolific over the past decade, this does not necessarily contradict the observation that the overall crime rate has fallen over the same period, as depicted by the British Crime Survey and other data sources (see Chapter 1,

---

33 Table 9.1, *Criminal Statistics England and Wales*, 1994 and 2001.

34 The Audit Commission work draws on Regional Drug Misuse (RDM) data to illustrate this growth. The rise in drug agencies' workloads, as reflected by RDM data, will partly reflect an increase in treatment capacity, but the rise is so large that it is unlikely to be a statistical artefact.

35 See also *Hammersley et al.* (2003) on substance use among young offenders.

above). This is because a larger proportion of crime may now be committed by a smaller pool of more hardened (and more drug dependent) offenders.

More serious offences

Whether offenders are committing more serious crimes – within the same offence categories – is very hard to test, as the crime figures do not shed any light on this.[36] As with arguments about more persistent offending there are reasons for thinking that offenders may be less controlled now than a decade ago – for example, if there is more drug-related offending, and if a greater proportion of this offending is linked to crack rather than heroin use. Excessive use of alcohol may also play an increasing part in some crimes, particularly violent crimes. Department of Health research found that the percentage of 16-24-year-old men drinking more than 28 units of alcohol per week rose from 22% to 32% between 1993 and 2001 (DoH, 2003); and Richardson et al. (2003) have observed a strong association between binge drinking and offending behaviour, especially of a violent nature.

In relation to sentencers' views on the seriousness of crime, only two conclusions can be drawn. First it would be rash and arrogant to reject out of hand the weight of opinion amongst magistrates and judges that the offences that they sentence have become more serious over the last 10 years. Secondly, even if this sense of worsening crime problems is largely grounded in the pessimism that years of contact with criminal justice may engender, the perception nevertheless may remain real in its consequences. If sentencers regard crimes as more serious than hitherto, one might expect them to hand out heavier sentences than hitherto.

In other words, sentencers' *perceptions* of the increased seriousness of crime – and, indeed, of increased persistence of offending – are undoubtedly a significant factor in sentencing practice, whatever the extent to which these perceptions are based on actual changes in offending behaviour. Moreover, sentencers' perceptions may themselves reflect the increased punitiveness of the general climate. This is because an emphasis – in society at large – on the culpability of offending behaviour may promote a more pessimistic view of individual offenders among sentencers. At the same time, the relationship may also work the other way: that is, the pessimism of the sentencers may feed into the broader punitiveness of the climate of opinion.

Respondents' views about trends in the nature of offences

Among the sentencers as a whole, increased seriousness of offending was by far the most popular explanation for the rise in the prison population. This was mentioned as a supplementary cause even by four of the five senior judges – who, as noted above, were more inclined than others to speak about their Crown Court colleagues' increasing severity. The senior judges argued for example that violent offences have become more violent; and that crimes related to dependent drug use have become more serious.

Thirteen of the fifteen Crown Court judges cited changing patterns of offending as a factor contributing to the rising prison population, at least seven of whom cited this unambiguously as the primary factor:

> *I think people are just becoming more lawless. I think it's probably a spreading thing that people think that they can get away [with it].* [Crown Court judge]

---

36 A study by Lloyd and Walmsley (1989) provides a rare example of research seeking to explore how the nature of a particular offence – namely, rape – had changed over time, and how any changes had been reflected in sentencing practice. The study concluded that in many respects the offence had changed little in terms of its 'nastiness' between 1973 and 1985 (despite the contentions of many judges and police officers that rapes were getting 'nastier'). Sentencing practice over this period had, however, become more severe. A recent paper by Ashworth (2002) on robbery illustrates the complexity of disentangling the various dimensions of this particular offence, and hence of assessing how it has changed over time. Robbery is a particularly broad offence category which encompasses, for example, professional and armed robberies of banks and security vans (which have declined in number) and robberies in the street involving small sums or items (which have increased). Offences of the latter kind are often on the borderline between robbery and theft from person.

The judges differed in how they described the changes in offending patterns. They spoke, variously, of a growth in crime in general; a growth in crime of a serious nature (such as violent or sexual offences or robberies); of certain kinds of crime becoming more serious (for example, violent offences becoming more violent). Several of the judges mentioned the impact of drugs on offending behaviour.

Similar views were expressed by the recorders: nine of the twelve talked about crime becoming more serious, of whom six described this as the primary cause of the growth in the prison population. Again, it was argued that the frequency and gravity of violent and other serious crimes have increased; and that illegal drugs are playing an ever-increasing role in offending behaviour, with the effect that much offending behaviour is more entrenched and takes more serious forms.

These themes were echoed also in the interviews with district judges and in the magistrates' focus groups. Ten of the 14 district judges spoke of changing patterns of offending, of whom six appeared to view this as the most important issue with respect to the current size of the prison population.

> *I think we're seeing more nastier work more often, particularly associated with drugs. My feeling is that there seems to be more violence now than there was, say, five years ago, very often drug connected. And when you've got that sort of scenario when other community penalties have been tried and failed then prison becomes inevitable.* [district judge]

> *In the magistrates' court I sense that one reason [for the increased prison population] may be that there is now a far greater proportion of persistent offenders appearing before the courts.* [district judge]

In talking about offending patterns, at least five of the district judges mentioned the highly prolific nature of much drug-related offending, which results in greater use of custody since offenders with long records, or who have breached previous community orders, are more likely to receive custodial sentences. In all 11 magistrates' focus groups, there was general agreement that changes in the scale and nature of offending have been *a* major, *or the* major, factor contributing to the rise in the prison population. In nine of the groups, for example, it was asserted that the amount or seriousness of violent crime has increased markedly in recent years. Increased persistence of offending was mentioned in six of the groups. The significance of drugs was stressed in six groups, and the impact of alcohol abuse on crime, and especially violent crime, was referred to in three groups.

Many sentencers – from senior judges to magistrates – talked about the impact of wider social changes on crime and disorder. Some suggested, for example, that a general decline in family values, moral standards, or respect for authority in wider society has contributed to high levels of lawlessness. In six of the magistrates' focus groups, and in interviews with one district judge, two recorders and one Crown Court judge, it was argued that offending by women has become more common and more serious in recent years[37] – reflecting a broader change in the status and self-perceptions of women in society.

---

37 Hedderman (2003) found that the available, if limited, evidence suggests offending by women has not increased in recent years; and that the number of women cautioned or found guilty dropped by 12 percentage points between 1992 and 2000. Gelsthorpe and Morris (2002) note that there have been some increases in crime committed by women, but these increases have not been dramatic and are mostly concentrated in the less serious crime categories.

Other factors

It is suggested above that increasing severity of sentencing is the primary explanation for the surge in the prison population since 1992, and that increased severity of offending, coupled with worsening criminal records, may be subsidiary factors. No claim is being made here that this is an exhaustive explanation. Many other factors have undoubtedly had some impact, some of which were identified by the respondents. These are summarised below, but no attempt has been made to quantify the extent to which they have contributed to the rise.

Changes in criminal procedure and practice

Over the decade there have been several changes to criminal procedure and practice. Several people identified changing practice on the part of the police and Crown Prosecution Service in decisions relating to charging. For example it was suggested that the CPS were winnowing out weaker cases, and less serious cases, whilst laying charges that had a more realistic chance of success. This would have the effect of increasing the average severity of cases in any particular crime category. In contrast some suggested that CPS over-charging sometimes brought cases to the Crown Court when they should have been dealt with by magistrates.

Changes in the availability of sentences and other facilities

Some judges and recorders argued that the restrictions on the use of suspended sentences imposed under the 1991 Criminal Justice Act had meant that they were using custody instead. This is consistent with the observation by Flood-Page and Mackie (1998: 125) that 'it seems highly likely that some cases which a few years ago would have attracted a suspended sentence have, by stages, moved to immediate custody'. Suspended sentences are discussed further in Chapter 5.

Some magistrates also commented on the lack of appropriate facilities for offenders with mental health problems, leading to the imposition of prison sentences.

Arrangements for supervision of community orders and recall of prisoners

Several respondents mentioned the increased rigour with which the conditions of community orders are now enforced, and the role that breach proceedings may have played in pushing up the prison population. Some thought that increased drugs problems had led to a growing number of breaches. It was also suggested that the Automatic Conditional Release (ACR) and Discretional Conditional Release (DCR) arrangements introduced by the 1991 Criminal Justice Act had led to a growing number of recalls in the second half of the sentence. The statistics on breached community penalties contained in successive *Probation Statistics* suggest that only a small proportion of the increase in the prison population can be attributed to imprisonment following breach proceedings, in situations where no further offending was involved.

Some judges suggested that Lord Chief Justice Taylor's 1992 Practice Statement, discussed in Chapter 2, regarding Automatic and Discretionary Conditional Release (ACR and DCR) had been overlooked with the passing of time. The ACR/DCR system that replaced parole for most prisoners meant that those eligible for release would serve a greater proportion of their nominal sentence (a minimum of a half rather than a third) than under the old arrangements. The direction required sentencers to adjust sentences downward to accommodate this. It was suggested that the direction's impact waned over time, and that by the mid-1990s sentences had floated back to their pre-1992 levels.

Increased detection of 'imprisonable' offences

There were various suggestions that changes in policing had affected the prison population. One was that the police were encouraging people to report offences liable to receive custodial sentences, such as rape. Others suggested that forensic techniques such as DNA testing were helping the police to catch more serious offenders. Both suggestions are plausible, but we cannot quantify their impact.

The rise in the prison population: an overview

Knowledge about factors driving up the adult prison population remains frustratingly sketchy. It can be said with certainty that the increase is not a product of rising crime. Nor are more people passing through the courts now than a decade ago. Rather, sentencers are making greater use of imprisonment than a decade ago and, when they do so, they tend to pass longer sentences. As illustrated in Chapter 2, above, the Crown Court was responsible for the surge in numbers in the early and mid-1990s; the magistrates' courts are implicated in the more recent rise.

An attempt has been made to analyse whether these trends reflect tougher decision-making, or more serious crimes and more culpable offenders, or both. The evidence is circumstantial but persuasive, nevertheless, that sentencers have toughened up over the last decade – with the result that, as has been observed by Morgan (2003:14) among others, 'more and more offenders are getting mired deeper and deeper within the criminal justice system for doing less and less'. This is in part a reflection of changes in the climate of opinion in which sentencers work, and partly a function of the legislative and legal frameworks within which they operate. Legislation, guideline judgements and sentence guidelines have all had an inflationary effect.

It is less clear whether the offenders appearing before the courts now tend to have longer criminal careers and to have committed more serious crimes than a decade ago. The statistical evidence for this is weak, but the views of sentencers themselves are strongly held and convincing – especially in the light of the growing prevalence of problematic drug and alcohol use. There is probably something in this argument, given the links between dependent drug use and offending, and between excessive alcohol consumption and violent crime; but further research is clearly needed to test it out more thoroughly.

In assessing sentencers' claims that tougher sentences reflect more serious offending, a sceptic would argue that 'they would say that, wouldn't they'. As will be discussed in the chapters that follow, sentencers firmly believe that they use custody only as an absolute last resort, and that they are not unduly swayed by the general climate of opinion. This implies consistency of practice over time. From the viewpoint of sentencers claiming consistency of practice, a 'last resort' in 1991 cannot be qualitatively different from one in 2001. Accordingly, they will be inclined to cite changes in crime, rather than changes in the broader sentencing environment and changes in their own decision-making, as the main determinant of sentencing trends.

In sum, the argument presented here is that the main factors behind the increase in the prison population are likely to be the following:

- A more punitive climate of opinion
- A more punitive legislative and legal sentencing framework
- Some changes in patterns of offending
- Sentencers' perceptions of changes in patterns of offending

These factors have undoubtedly interacted with each other; hence it can be said that the growth in the prison population has emerged out of the *interplay* between them. These are unlikely to prove the only factors at play, however; several others have been listed above which may have had a subsidiary effect.

4 Sentencing decisions

With no single cause of the rise in the prison population, there is unlikely to be a single effective way of reversing the rise. In an ideal world the best approach would be to reduce further the numbers of crimes that are committed. There are many possible approaches to doing so, but it is well beyond the scope of this study to consider these. In so far as sentencers reflect the climate of opinion about crime and punishment, any attempt to change sentencing practice is unlikely to be successful in isolation: it would make sense to try to achieve some shift towards a less punitive social and political climate.

Nevertheless, the core of any strategy to contain prison numbers will be concerned directly with sentencing decisions, and in particular with the decisions *whether* to imprison and *how long* to imprison. Any attempt to change sentencers' decision-making will require a proper understanding of the decision process. This and the next two chapters present findings about how these decisions are made, and about factors taken into account by sentencers when making their decisions. This chapter focuses on the decision whether or not to sentence someone to custody.

Prison as a last resort

Sentencers participating in this study were asked both about their general approach to sentencing, and about how they make decisions in relation to cases on the borderline between custody and community sentences, referred to here as 'cusp cases'.[38] Crown Court judges, recorders, district judges and magistrates stressed time and again that they use custody only as a last resort, as they are required by legislation. Typical comments included:

> *We do try to keep people out of prison if at all possible.* [Crown Court judge]

> *I bend over backwards to avoid custody.* [recorder]

> *The last thing in the world that I think about is sending somebody to prison.* [district judge]

> *Custody is a last option, and indeed is one rarely given. When a custodial sentence is given, it is because there is no other sanction applicable.* [magistrate: questionnaire response]

As discussed in the last chapter, there are pressures on sentencers to give accounts of their decisions that are rational and consistent. Like most people, they will think of themselves as humane and civilized. So at one level it would be surprising if sentencers did not talk in terms of prison as a last resort. However the sincerity with which these views were expressed was striking. Some of them emphasised the difficulty and distaste they felt in imposing a custodial sentence. For example, a magistrate in a focus group commented that when an offender is sent to custody, "…it is something that you will reflect, that you have taken the responsibility with a couple of others of depriving someone of their liberty". A recorder spoke of being "incredibly loath" to sentence someone to prison; he remarked also that the very act of sentencing is "a peculiarly naked and direct form of exercising power over somebody".

---

38 Crown Court judges, recorders and district judges were asked in interview to describe four 'cusp cases', two of which had led to custodial sentences and two of which had resulted in community sentences, and the key factors that had tipped their decisions towards or away from the custody. A similar exercise was included in the magistrates' questionnaire. Details were received from sentencers on a total of 311 cusp cases (of which 163 were provided in the magistrates' questionnaire). 150 of the 311 cases went to custody or were committed to Crown Court from magistrates' courts for sentence; 161 resulted in non-custodial sentences.

Borderline/cusp cases

Respondents' comments on the sentencing of cusp cases illustrate what the use of custody as a 'last resort' means in practice. These cases covered a wide range of offences, the most common of which were offences of violence (of widely varying degrees of seriousness[39]) and motoring offences (including driving while disqualified, dangerous driving, and driving with excess alcohol). Theft and handling (including several cases of theft in breach of trust), dwelling and non-dwelling burglary, and fraud and forgery cases were also common. No pattern was discernible with respect to the kinds of cases that fell into the custodial and non-custodial brackets.

Whilst there were no consistent differences between the offence categories which comprised custody cases and those attracting community penalties, there were marked differences in the sorts of factors which tipped the decision one way or the other. In the majority of cusp cases that resulted in *custody*, sentencers' decisions were based on two considerations:

- the kind or nature of the offence was deemed so serious that no other sentence was possible, and/or

- the offender's past convictions and failure to respond to past sentences ruled out non-custodial options.[40]

The latter played a particularly important part in many of the cusp cases dealt with by magistrates and district judges. Thus it is clear that, in practice, the concept of the 'last resort' has two possible meanings for sentencers: first, it can refer to the seriousness of the offence itself; secondly, it can refer to the past history of the offender, who may be convicted for a relatively minor offence but is deemed to have run out of options because of the number of past convictions.

In contrast, a wider range of factors were of greatest significance in cusp cases resulting in *non-custodial sentences*. Issues relating to the present circumstances and condition of the offender were viewed as particularly important in such cases. So too were the offender's response to prosecution and his or her status as being 'of previous good character'. Hence the factors most frequently cited in non-custodial cases were the following:

Response to prosecution

- Demonstration of genuine remorse, or the capacity to understand the repercussions of the criminal act

- Guilty plea

- Evidence of co-operation with the courts and probation

Condition of the offender

- Evidence of motivation to address problems causing offending behaviour (drugs, drink, violent tendencies and so on)

- Treatable psychiatric problems

- Medical problems

- Age (young offender or middle aged/elderly offender)

---

39 Though typically the offenders were charged with Section 20 (malicious wounding/grievous bodily harm) or Section 47 (actual bodily harm) assaults.

40 Parker et al.'s research on the sentencing of young offenders by magistrates (1989) likewise found that the seriousness of the offence and the offender's criminal record were frequently cited in decisions to impose custody. Other factors that were accorded particular significance were a perceived need for public protection, and a negative moral assessment of the offender. Similar findings also emerged from Flood-Page and Mackie's study of sentencing practice in magistrates' courts and the Crown Court (1998). They found that the factors most commonly associated with custodial decisions were: risk to the public; a planned or unprovoked offence; the infliction of serious injury; a vulnerable victim; previous convictions; an offence committed when the offender was subject to a court order.

Situation of the offender

- Family responsibilities (for children or elderly/disabled relatives)
- Support from family, especially parents
- Stable relationship with partner
- Current employment/training or prospects of employment/training
- Positive references from employers or other
- Accommodation

Criminal history

- No previous convictions; no recent convictions; no related previous convictions

Thus personal mitigation, of the kinds outlined above, appears to play the largest part in tipping a sentencing decision away from custody. To a lesser extent, mitigating factors relating to the offence itself were also cited as factors in the decisions to avoid custody. Table 4.1 provides a breakdown of the factors cited in custodial and non-custodial cusp cases.

Table 4.1. Factors considered in 311 cusp cases by sentencers

Factors[1]	Custodial cases					Non-custodial cases				
	Mags	DJs	Rs	Js	total	Mags	DJs	Rs	Js	total
Nature of offence[2]	42	18	18	13	91	18	4	5	12	39
Criminal history	45	13	4	9	71	31	8	9	10	58
Response to prosecution	13	3	6	5	27	31	6	15	9	61
Offender's situation	5	1	3	-	9	29	10	19	13	71
Offender's condition	4	2	3	-	9	28	19	14	12	73
Other[3]	10	7	10	7	34	21	10	12	16	60

Notes (1) Key factors which tipped decision towards or away from custody
(2) Seriousness of the offence, including offence-related aggravating or mitigating factors
(3) Includes reference to need to send a 'message' about certain offences, perceived risk of reoffending, PSR recommendations and other factors

The emphasis on personal mitigation in non-custodial cusp cases is reflected in the process of decision-making undertaken by sentencers. It emerged in the interviews that this process is not necessarily highly structured for sentencers other than magistrates.[41] Nevertheless, a sentencer tends first to make a decision about whether or not an offence, in its own terms, merits custody; if it does, but is not well over the custody threshold, the sentencer will then consider whether personal mitigation can pull it down from custody to a community sentence. As one recorder said:

> *Quite often you read [the case papers] and think, well this chap's got to go inside, and then you ... hear all the mitigating circumstances and you come down on a non-custodial. [recorder]*

Hence in several accounts of cusp cases, sentencers commented that an offence 'on the face of it' pointed to custody; but other factors then led to a decision to opt for a non-custodial sentence. As noted above, concerns relating to the offender can pull a decision towards as well as away from custody, in the sense that criminal history is often a determining factor in a decision to impose a prison sentence (particularly in the magistrates' courts). However, the

---

41 When asked in the focus groups about how they make sentencing decisions, magistrates tended to say that they follow a structured process, and make full use of their sentencing guidelines. (90% of questionnaire respondents likewise stated that they refer to the guidelines when retiring, and none stated that they make little or no use of guidelines.) In contrast, the other sentencers were more likely to say that the decision-making process is intuitive, at least to some degree.

typical pattern in the cusp cases described by the sentencers was that characteristics of the offence placed the offender at risk of custody, and characteristics of the offender provided mitigation where custody was rejected.

In one of the magistrates' focus groups, there was a marked divergence from the otherwise pervasive view that personal mitigation can easily tip a sentencing decision away from custody. This group stressed that they had been encouraged to make their decisions about custody with regard only to the offence itself, and not with regard to its aggravating or mitigating features. (It was not made clear where this advice had come from.) Mitigating features relating to the offender, they said, could reduce the length of a custodial sentence, but would be unlikely to alter a decision to impose custody. This was described by the magistrates themselves as a 'hardening' of their approach to sentencing, which, they said, coincided with the introduction about 12 months previously of a 'structured sentencing form' which was used to guide decision-making. Not surprisingly this bench was above average in its use of custody.

The 'unavoidability' of custody

Sentencers are aware of current concerns about the size of the prison population, and of the view within Government and the senior judiciary that custody, and particularly short sentences, should be used as sparingly as possible. Some mentioned the guideline judgements of *Mills* and *Kefford*. However, as noted above, the overall and strong message from the sentencers who took part in this study was that they already use custody sparingly: that they resort to custodial sentences only when the seriousness of the offences and/or the offenders' records leave them no other option. They stressed also that this applies to short sentences as much as longer sentences: that is, they impose short sentences because they are compelled to do so by the nature or circumstances of the offence, and not because they believe these sentences are likely to be constructive for the offender.

Many of the sentencers commented that short sentences achieve little or nothing as far as individual offenders are concerned, other than for those who might be new enough to the criminal justice system to be shocked by the 'clang of the prison gate'. (In such cases, it was observed, no more than a few days or weeks inside may be appropriate.) On the other hand, many sentencers made the point that the short prison sentence is an important part of the armoury of the sentencer, because it enables him or her to mark the gravity of certain forms of offending behaviour. One district judge, for example, said that while he "wouldn't pretend for one minute that any prison sentence you can pass in a magistrates' court can have any rehabilitative effect", a short sentence does allow the sentencer to show the public "that if they put their hands in the fire they get burnt". It was also pointed out that short sentences at least have the effect of removing highly prolific offenders from the general chaos of their lives for a period, and taking them out of circulation:

> *I don't think even sentencers are naïve enough to actually claim [short sentences] do anything in terms of rehabilitation. It locks people up, and in many respects, that's the best outcome at this moment in time you can get for a lot of people. It just keeps them away from those who they're causing problems to.* [district judge]

Sentencers express widespread support for proposals for 'Custody Plus' in the Review of the Sentencing Framework (Home Office, 2001): that is, a new custodial sentence of up to three months followed by a period of supervision in the community. Provisions for this sentence were contained in the Criminal Justice Bill before Parliament at the time of writing.[42] Custody Plus aims to overcome some of the problems hitherto associated with short sentences, through its combination of custodial and community-based elements. Sentencers' approval of the proposed sentence thus accords with their general view that short custodial sentences are a necessary but problematic sentencing option. However, some of the respondents sounded a note of caution, pointing out that Custody Plus might come to be viewed as the 'easy option' by sentencers; it could substitute for community penalties rather than conventional custody, and serve to accelerate the increase in the prison population.

Given their insistence that they already use custody only as an absolute last resort, it is no surprise that many of the sentencers were resistant to the idea that they should reduce their use of custody in order to reverse the rise in the prison population. For example, magistrates in one of the focus groups argued that to allow concerns about the prison population to constrain sentencing options would be a case of 'the tail wagging the dog', since sentencing should be about ensuring that 'the punishment fits the crime'. This point was echoed by other magistrates and many district judges, and, to a lesser extent, some of the Crown Court judges and recorders. For example:

> *It isn't our problem, it shouldn't be magistrates' problem at all, it's the Home Office's problem and that's it. ... a lot of thought goes into it before somebody goes to prison, but if that's the sentence then whether prison is full or no, it goes to prison it's as simple as that.* [magistrate]

> *Sentencing guidelines exist in order to protect the public, not to reduce the prison population. [district judge]*

> *There is public alarm ...that the Government is saying we don't have enough room in prison therefore people who would otherwise merit going to prison won't go.* [recorder]

> *I think it's wrong in principle that people that commit crime for which they should be receiving a custodial sentence escape because there is not sufficient room to contain them.* [Crown Court judge]

The most forceful articulation of the need for recourse to custodial sentences was made by a district judge, who commented that while he appreciates the fact that the prisons are 'crammed full', he would like to see the Lord Chief Justice and others visit a magistrates' court:

> *... which is the engine room? The Crown Court isn't the engine room, the Court of Appeal isn't the engine room, the House of Lords isn't the engine room – <u>this</u> is the factory floor. If, with respect to them, they come and see the large volume of cases, what goes on in a magistrates' court, they would know that the right message in certain cases to be sent out is custody. End of story.*

The narratives of sentencing

It was evident from the ways in which the sentencers described their cusp cases that sentencing is not so much a technical or value-neutral process as a value-laden process of constructing and exploring the narratives of the lives of the people in the dock. The case studies below illustrate this narrative aspect of sentencing. This, of course, reflects the fact that

---

42 While sentencers were generally enthusiastic about Custody Plus, they may have to wait some time before they can use it. According to the Criminal Justice Bill Team at the Home Office (correspondence April 2003) the Probation Service in particular will need to be well resourced to deal with the new sentences introduced under the Bill, and especially with Custody Plus. It is expected that the various sentencing measures will be introduced in phases to enable the Service to reach the capacity needed. Custody Plus is likely to be one of the last sentences to be rolled out. No decisions have yet been made about whether it will be piloted before it is fully implemented.

the court process as a whole – especially when there is a trial – centres on the complex human stories of the offenders and those affected by their actions, as much as on the law. But perhaps the narrative aspect of sentencing is also an inevitable corollary of the emphasis placed, in sentencing decisions, on the personal situations, histories and attitudes of offenders.

Case study 1: Cusp case leading to custodial sentence (district judge decision)

This was a case of domestic violence. The offender was a man in his 40s, who pleaded guilty to the offence, and to breaching a conditional discharge received with respect to an offence of criminal damage against the girlfriend's property. He also had previous convictions for violence against his girlfriend, and a previous conviction for grievous bodily harm dating back to the 1980s.

The offence had taken place one evening, when he had gone out with his girlfriend in an attempt to repair a rift between them. After drinking too much, he assaulted her: grabbing her hair, forcing her to the floor, and punching her three times in the back of the head. She suffered bruising, and attended hospital.

The offender was sentenced to a six-week custodial sentence for the assault and a 14-day consecutive sentence for the breach. Custody was deemed to be inevitable because of the seriousness of the offence (the violence was domestic, and it was a bad assault), and because of the offender's criminal history, including recent violence and criminal damage aimed at the same victim.

Mitigating factors considered by the sentencer were the offender's demonstration of remorse and an impassioned plea from the girlfriend against a custodial sentence. On these grounds, the sentence was made as short as possible.

Case study 2: Cusp case leading to non-custodial sentence (recorder decision)

A postman was convicted of the theft of a number of cheques taken from the mail. The theft therefore involved a breach of trust.

The sentencer in this case noted that the Court of Appeal has said that postal staff who steal from the mail should expect to go straight to custody. However, he made the decision here to impose a Community Punishment Order of the maximum duration (240 hours). From a strictly legal point of view, the sentencer observed, he could be said to have 'let the side down'.

The decision to pass a non-custodial sentence was taken on the grounds that the circumstances of the case were such that it was justifiable to 'go out on the limb'. These circumstances were the following:

- The offender had not cashed the cheques, but had kept them and was contemplating making use of them. He had evidently felt himself to be in a 'moral dilemma' over what he had done.
- He committed the offence at a time when he faced severe social and financial problems.
- He was a man of hitherto good character.
- He was very remorseful, and had entered an early guilty plea.
- Probation had provided a very supportive pre-sentence report.
- He was the father of three children.

Case study 3: Cusp case leading to non-custodial sentence (Crown Court judge decision)

The offender in this case was a 31-year-old man, convicted of handling stolen credit cards (with which he had bought £3,000-worth of electrical goods for Christmas presents). He had a long record of dishonesty offences; a year before committing this offence he had been released on licence from a lengthy prison sentence.

The sentencer in this case commented that, 'on the face of it', it had been a case for custody because of the offender's previous convictions and the fact that he had breached his licence conditions. However, the judge decided to pass a Community Punishment Order, primarily on the grounds that since the offender had been released from prison he had, on the whole, 'done incredibly well' for a man with his record. His life had settled: he was back living with his family, and his use of drugs was under control. The decision to impose a CPO was also encouraged by the pre-sentence report, which noted that this would be a suitable disposal.

The judge reserved any breaches of the community order to himself – telling the offender that if he did not take the opportunity he had been offered, he would face custody.

This emphasis on the personal undoubtedly makes the sentencing process a highly subjective one, in which the individual sentencer (or group of sentencers, in the case of magistrates) has to assess the intentions and capabilities of the offender and his or her attitude towards the offence, and offending, such as the presence or absence of remorse and the determination to stop offending. These assessments feed judgements about responsibility and culpability. In other words, sentencers' decisions are framed within a set of explicitly ethical concepts. Occasionally sentencers use the terminology of morality; one recorder, for example, commented that he decided not to use custody in a particular case because 'prison is for evil people', and the offender in question was 'not evil'.

In cusp decisions, it was clear that sentencers were casting around for some reason to avoid a custodial sentence. This could be an indication – of any kind – that a prolific offender was willing and able to change his or her offending behaviour, or that a first-time offender would not offend again. In a sense, therefore, the process of sentencing of cusp cases can become a search for hope – even a glimmer of hope – that can justify a non-custodial sentence.

Hence, for example, it was common for sentencers to refer to 'remorse' or 'contrition' as a factor that could tip them away from a custodial sentence, even if the offence in itself might otherwise merit custody. In such cases, of course, they would have to be convinced that the remorse was 'genuine': a senior judge, for example, spoke of looking at an offender and having to decide if:

> ... he's blubbing away there and the only reason he's blubbing away is that he's sorry for himself; or look at him: he does actually realise that this has had a devastating effect on the victim.

In several of the cusp cases, reference was made to the fact that the offence in question was a 'one-off' and 'out of character', based on the sentencer's assumption that the offender was essentially a law-abiding individual who had acted under extreme stress or in a 'stupid moment' or 'moment of madness'. In such cases, evidence of remorse played a particularly important part in convincing the sentencer that this was an offence that would never be repeated.

Signs of hope for offenders may stem not only from their response to prosecution, but also from other aspects of their lives. Sentencers often spoke of such developments as the mending of a relationship with parents, a new boyfriend or girlfriend who might bring stability to a hitherto chaotic life, or prospects of a job or training, as critical factors in a decision to opt for a community sentence. The thinking here would be that life-changes of this sort might make an offender more able to comply with, and learn from, a community order. An existing job and home, family support, or family responsibilities, are likewise viewed as encouraging aspects of an offender's life: again, they may improve chances of success of a community order, partly because the offender has more to lose if he or she fails. Most obviously, evidence that an offender is already taking steps to address the problems that caused the offending behaviour – for example, by undertaking voluntary drug or alcohol treatment, or where there are convincing reports from probation that prior work with the offender is progressing well – can provide the basis for a decision to avoid custody.

The converse of the situation where signs of hope can be found is the situation in which community options have been used and failed before, and, in the view of the sentencer, there is nothing to suggest that a non-custodial sentence would be any more successful the next time. This is when, in the words of a district judge, courts find themselves "out of despair using custody". Magistrates in one focus group talked of people who are "sentencing themselves', because of their past failures to respond; likewise, it was observed in one of the magistrates' questionnaires that custody is used "as the last option when all else has failed (and has been seen to have failed)".

The inevitable subjectivity of the process of assessing hope or failure can help to explain sharp inconsistencies in sentencing practice between sentencers who all assert that they use custody only as an absolute last resort. In other words, what constitutes the last resort is a relative rather than an absolute concept. It was notable that while the magistrates' benches included in this study were selected on the basis that they had contrasting custody rates, magistrates in all the focus groups generally spoke in very similar terms about their use of custody. This is perhaps not surprising since, clearly, what is a last resort for one sentencer (or bench, if a bench culture has developed) will not necessarily be the last resort for another – as the latter may typically perceive something in an offender's life to be a glimmer of hope that the former dismisses as irrelevant or does not even notice.[43]

Another implication of the emphasis on personal mitigation in cusp decisions is the differential impact that this has on offenders from different socio-economic groups. Since having a job, home and family are frequently cited as factors militating against custody, offenders who are already socially and economically disadvantaged are likely to suffer further disadvantage in the sentencing process. Other aspects of sentencing can enhance this disparity. For example, two or three of the sentencers suggested that in some cases the stress and repercussions of being prosecuted – especially for a middle class or previously well-respected individual and his or

---

43 Parker et al. observed, with respect to magistrates' sentencing of young offenders, that sentencers relied very much on their personal judgement of the defendant's character. It is no wonder that sentencing patterns are so difficult to explain when at the heart of the process is the belief that sentencers, and they alone, are uniquely placed to understand not only the uniqueness of the events which constitute the offence, but also the character of the individual who has committed it (1989: 116).

her family – are so severe that a custodial sentence can be avoided on the grounds that the offender has already 'suffered enough'. One Crown Court judge noted, for example, that

> *I always give big credit to middle-aged persons of previous good character on the basis that they are unlikely to commit an offence again and will have found a court appearance a genuinely stressful event.*

It was also suggested that a non-custodial sentence may be used where the effects of custody would be 'disproportionate' because it would lead to the loss of a job and home. One recorder added, having made this kind of point, that "this is probably how the middle class offender so often gets away without custody".

5 Alternatives to custody

One of the main working hypotheses used in designing this study was that increased use of imprisonment reflected dissatisfaction with the community-based alternatives. The study was envisaged as a sort of market research exercise that would identify weaknesses in the community penalty 'product'. More attractive packages of community alternatives could then be designed to tempt sentencers away from their use of short prison sentences.

One of the study's more important findings is that this working hypothesis was simplistic. Sentencers did not identify a lack of satisfactory community options as a factor tipping decisions towards custody. According to the analysis of cusp cases, only in two of 150 cases that went to custody was a lack of community options cited as a key factor in the sentencing decision.[44] One was a case of shoplifting, committed while the offender was on bail, and dealt with by a district judge. The district judge noted that the offender had been sentenced to custody 'on default', because the pre-sentence report observed that probation could not 'come up with anything imaginative' with respect to this individual. The other case was a complex one involving persistent harassment, which culminated in the offender dousing himself in petrol in front of his ex-partner and threatening to kill himself. The judge had pressed the probation service to locate a suitable anger management programme, but none could be found.

As discussed in Chapter 4, the sentencers involved in this study stressed their use of custody only as a 'last resort'. They were therefore insistent that they already use community sentences wherever possible. However, this is not to suggest that sentencers' confidence in the probation service and in the existing range of community sentences on offer is irrelevant to cusp decisions.

Sentencers' views of the Probation Service

Historically sentencers had somewhat mixed views of probation effectiveness. One senior judge noted: 'Every judge you speak to has had experience of going for the probation option and coming unstuck with it.' Similarly, during one of the focus groups a magistrate commented that: "Ten to fifteen years ago I would have said no, but I have to say now, in my experience, that the [local] Probation Service … are excellent, they've improved no end."

There was widespread agreement that the Probation Service had improved in recent years and, in particular, that enforcement had 'toughened-up' following the introduction of National Standards:

> *They've clearly changed their act in relation to breach, they're under National Standards of course. They are clearly under greater scrutiny about their breach processes.*
> [district judge]

> *[Probation is rigourous in enforcing conditions] … under the new National Standards. They didn't used to be, they used to be abysmal before …* [magistrate]

---

44 In the cusp case section of the magistrates' questionnaire, respondents were prompted for "availability (or lack of availability) of [community] programmes or services as one factor (among others) that could shape a decision about whether or not to impose custody." Despite this prompt, lack of availability was not cited by any magistrate as a factor in a custodial cusp case.

On the whole, the sentencers also spoke highly of the provision of community sentences by the Probation Service. They were also, by and large, happy with the quality of the Pre-Sentence Reports (PSRs) they received – for example:

> *There has been a sea change in the kinds of PSRs that are produced – they are now more realistic and argue their case.* [recorder]

Thus there was general satisfaction among the sentencers with the work carried out by probation – in terms of enforcement, the provision of community orders, and PSRs. Not all views were so positive, of course. One magistrate thought there was poor communication between the service and his bench. Some doubts about enforcement were expressed by some of the sentencers, including one recorder who clearly did not believe that probation was as strict as it might be in enforcing National Standards:

> *One's always anxious that probation are too slow to breach. They insist they're not. But when you see some of the programmes, you find sometimes that they provide for three or more defaults before any warning is issued. I regard that as too many.*[45]

More broadly, there was evidence of regional and court variation in terms of sentencers' relationships with probation and in the service's ability to perform its functions while being limited by funds and staffing. Indeed, many of the sentencers voiced their concern that the service was hindered by a lack of funding and personnel. A typical focus group discussion on the subject is shown below:

Magistrates focus group – Are you happy with the Probation Service?

R1 *I think they've improved in the last 10 years. The Probation Service has changed beyond recognition.*

R2 *But it's been tightened up hasn't it?*

R3 *They need more resources.*

R4 *Oh I think they have, only when they use accredited programmes, they're tried and tested and they really work. I still think more can be done but I think… I think they're really on the right track.*

R3 *They're on the right track but they need more support, more resources.*

R4 *More resources, they're stretched to the limit.*

The firm belief among many of the sentencers that the Probation Service suffered from a lack of resources was, it seems, partly based on their experiences of delays in receiving PSRs. One district judge, for example, said that he rarely received PSRs within three weeks due to the Probation Service's lack of staff. It was also occasionally suggested that under-staffing meant that the supervision of offenders on community orders was not as intensive as it should have been.

Do sentencers want feedback on cases?

When asked if sentencers received enough feedback from probation one senior judge said: "The answer to your question is they don't. And the answer to your next question is that they

---

45 National Standards 2000 dictate that two unacceptable absences (including one warning) are permitted before breach proceedings are initiated.

should. "There was general support for the principle of improving feedback, although no real consensus as to whether this should be in the form of information on individual cases, aggregated statistics, or both.

That said, 80% of magistrates who completed the questionnaire said they would like feedback on individual cases, while only a quarter said they currently received this. This of course did not indicate whether the Probation Service was at fault for failing to provide the information, or the individual magistrate for failing to ask for it.[46] Sixty per cent said they would like more 'general' feedback on the impact of sentences. Typical responses are outlined below:

Magistrates' questionnaire responses – views on feedback on cases

Case-specific feedback:

1.   *When a community penalty has been imposed 'by a whisker.'*

2.   *Where community sentences have been imposed when the defendant has failed to respond to prison sentence.*

3.   *In mode of trial decisions, if we send to Crown Court and [the defendant] is found guilty. It would help to know what sentence was given by the judge.*

Statistical feedback:

1.   *It would be useful to know which types of community penalty were more effective and which the least.*

2.   *Perhaps not on exact details but information on bench performance would be more useful.*

3.   *Feedback on the success of probation programmes.*

While some magistrates said they already received feedback (usually via probation liaison committees) this was clearly not reaching everyone. There was also concern among some sentencers as to the effect extra requests for feedback would have on probation:

> *[A judge in this court] wants reports on everybody he puts on probation, ... but if we all wanted that, it would put a bit of a burden on the Probation Service. So the only time we know is when something's gone wrong. Occasionally they do apply to discharge the order early because things have gone well. So in that way we get some feedback.*
> **[Crown Court judge]**

Others also made the point that they usually hear only about those community orders which have failed in one way or another; and that wider feedback (either individual or aggregate) would therefore be helpful in that it would provide a more balanced view of the outcome of community sentences. One Crown Court judge commented that he would find extra feedback useful, but not necessarily the burden of any extra work involved.

Does current provision need to be redesigned?

While many sentencers are happy with the current provision of community penalties, areas for improvement were identified. Those that specifically commented on Community Rehabilitation Orders (CROs; formerly probation orders) were generally positive, particularly when work was done through accredited programmes. One district judge took the view that

---

46 A Home Office study of community sentences (Hedderman *et al.*, 1999) found that most sentencers said they wanted individual feedback but did not ask for it. It is suggested that this may be because they wanted information on certain cases about which they were particularly concerned, but not about all cases. The sentencers were also eager to receive aggregate feedback on the completion of programmes and reconviction rates.

CROs were taken seriously by defendants, especially if given with conditions. This said, a recorder thought more structure might be needed and in one area a district judge noted drift in some programmes.

Although many were happy with Community Punishment Orders (CPOs; formerly community service orders), there is scope for making them tougher. One recorder thought that CPOs, as they currently are, would not put someone off crime. A district judge commented that the orders were not especially difficult:

> *I doubt whether the work undertaken under Community Punishment Orders is particularly onerous or arduous. ... The value of it, perhaps, is in relation to those who haven't got a work pattern. [district judge]*

One recorder thought that the order should be based on a full 40 hour week. Other sentencers thought that the option of making CPOs longer should be available. Some magistrates suggested that offenders on CPOs should be more 'visible' in the community, a few even arguing that they should be made to wear orange jackets or uniforms.

While most sentencers were quite happy to use CROs, CPOs and CPROs (combined CROs and CPOs, formerly combination orders), some also thought these could be improved in terms of quality and quantity. A district judge observed that, in his view, a high percentage of defendants will offend again, sometimes during the order. Two of the Crown Court judges interviewed had similar doubts about community penalties working. However, they were prepared to suspend their disbelief in order to sentence, taking the view that they should not be constrained by what works or what does not work; in the words of one Crown Court judge, "if it falls within the range I pass it, regardless of how effective it would be." Another was more explicit about setting aside his scepticism:

> *I have my doubts about CPOs, but in practice I put them entirely out of my mind. The system exists and they are there to punish – and I use them for that purpose. [Crown Court judge]*

Sentencers had mixed views of curfew orders (with electronic tagging), largely dependent on their level of experience with them.[47] Comments by some of the sentencers interviewed for this study indicated that there is wide variation in availability and usage of curfew orders:

> *I think I've only used a curfew order once and as far as I'm aware they're not very widely used by ... certainly by the adult bench at all. ... We haven't made widespread use of those at all. [magistrate]*

In the same focus group another magistrate commented that: "They never seem to fit in with our sort or type [of defendant]." In areas where curfew orders were used more regularly they were viewed as demanding on the offender. As an alternative to prison, they were often seen as being "as close to custody as you get." (Crown Court judge) One district judge said he had confidence in using a curfew "because it is monitored and breach proceedings are taken." He went on to observe:

> *I certainly see the curfew as equivalent [to custody] as it deprives the defendant of a considerable degree of liberty during, perhaps, a substantial period in any 24 hours.*

---

47 Research has shown that the initial uptake of the order by sentencers was low during the first pilots (Mair and Mortimer, 1996) and in the early stages of the national roll-out (Walter, 2002; Walter, Sugg and Moore, 2001), reflecting a lack of knowledge about and confidence in the new penalty. However, take-up has grown over time. The national evaluation also found that PSRs infrequently recommended curfew orders (Walter, 2002).

One problem with curfews, observed by a Crown Court judge, was the 'bureaucratic process' involved in getting them back to court after breach. The same of course can be said for most other community orders.

Most sentencers were positive about DTTOs, with one district judge claiming they have been the most effective community penalty of the past ten years. Magistrates were similarly enthusiastic, with 64% of those who completed the questionnaire saying they would like to visit a DTTO programme. Despite this, resourcing and supervision problems were identified in some areas which has had a knock-on effect on confidence:

> *Well I mean we've had a serious problem with DTTOs because they've not been adequately supervised and so this has to a certain extent broken the bench's faith in them.* [magistrate]

In this example, the magistrate did go on to say the problem had been addressed "…because the agency that was actually administering them has been replaced." According to some sentencers, there is scope for further increasing confidence in DTTOs by providing more residential orders. There was general approval of the DTTO review process, although there was also some frustration that this does not allow for breach:

> *The difficulty is, if you come back on a review and the person has done absolutely hopelessly, … you cannot do anything with them. They can only be brought back by the service on a breach. It would be nice to be able to threaten them with something so there's a bit of stick along with the carrot.* [Crown Court judge]

Are more non-custodial options needed?

Sentencers were divided in opinion as to whether any new non-custodial sentences were required. Several of the respondents suggested that there had been too many new initiatives over recent years.[48] One magistrate commented in a focus group: "I suppose we'd just like them to keep the same things for a couple of years." A district judge expressed similar views:

> *… no sooner do you start to understand what you've got then we've got another wedge of legislation. The system's clogged with it. …I think, actually, the Government ought to try and give the criminal justice system a pause for breath without changing the rules every few minutes.*

Despite this, some sentencers did call for new orders and new powers which, they claimed, could reduce reliance on custody. However, there was no general consensus on the question of what was needed. One recorder called for a more fundamental change in sentencing practice, with emphasis being placed on compensating the victim, treating crimes more like torts. Other sentencers just wanted more 'tough' alternatives to custody. Possibilities suggested by magistrates and district judges (forms of which are in fact already provided for) include:

- Wider powers to restrict people's movement [district judge]
- Education Orders that teach basic skills [magistrate]
- Alcohol Treatment Orders [magistrate]

---

48 The Home Office evaluation of curfew orders similarly found that practitioners have felt inundated by new initiatives (Walter, Sugg and Moore, 2001).

- Residential Rehabilitation Centres – to act as a half-way house between custody and community sentences [magistrate and district judge]
- Secure facilities for people with mental health problems [magistrate]

One consistent recommendation from the professional judiciary was a call for greater use of suspended sentences. One senior judge believed that it had been a mistake to restrict the use of suspended sentences to exceptional circumstances, commenting that:

> *[The Government's] purpose I think was, that if you don't pass a suspended sentence you deal with them some other way, but they didn't expect that other way to be custody. ...They also did away with partly suspended sentences.* [senior judge]

The Criminal Justice Bill (2003) includes provision for the combination of a community order with a suspended sentence – termed 'Custody Minus' in the White Paper *Justice for All* (2002). There was some support for this idea – although awareness of the proposal itself seemed limited. One prescient or well-informed district judge thought that a new community penalty which came with a suspended prison sentence and a DTTO-type review would be useful.[49] He was not alone in suggesting the use of suspended prison sentences with community penalties:

> *It's a great pity that we can't now use suspended sentences in conjunction with other sentences in the appropriate cases. I think if you're doing a community sentence with a custodial sentence hanging over you, it must have an effect. It's coming now, but too late.* [Crown Court judge]

The sentencer-defendant contract

As mentioned earlier, there was enthusiasm for the DTTO review process. Some sentencers suggested extending this to other sentences. This form of sentencer-defendant contract was widely believed to be beneficial:

> *Anything that keeps you linked to the defendant, ... or keeps the offender linked to the court helps, it helps him, it gives him the idea that he's, in effect, truly [his emphasis] on probation. It's not a let-off, he's truly being attached to the court, the court's continuing to be interested in him.* [senior judge]

As things currently stand, in practical terms this can only be achieved via DTTO reviews, or by attempting to reserve breach hearings to the sentencing judge. Turnbull *et al.* (2000:52) found the DTTO review process to be both positive and productive if heard by the original sentencer. While it cannot be guaranteed that breach hearings are heard by the original judge, some sentencers do attempt this. When they do, some make a particular point of it when summing up:

> *What I tend to do is ... if I think I've taken a bit of a risk with somebody, ... I reserve breaches to myself. ... I say something like 'I'm asking for reports on you. They will come every three months. ...You breach this order, you will come back in front of me, because it's coming to me and nobody else'... It's all a bit of drama and showmanship but I like to think that you're impressing something ... that they are a bit frightened of the consequences of breaching.* [Crown Court judge]

---

49 The Criminal Justice Bill contains provisions for exactly this.

Such a contract with the offender is seen as positive in terms of ensuring compliance and in demonstrating the court's interest in the defendant. The next logical step is to extend this to include the victim, as in the restorative justice model.[50] While none of the sentencers suggested this directly, one Crown Court judge did mention the possible benefits of encouraging a "confrontation with victims".

---

50 See Miers (2001) for a useful international review of restorative justice. See also Hoyle, Young and Hill (2002) and Miers et al. (2001) for examples of work done in the UK.

6 The political and social context

All the sentencers interviewed for this study were acutely aware that their sentencing decisions are not made in a vacuum, but in a highly pressured political and social context. Respondents were asked how they saw the political pressures on them, and how they experienced media pressure and public opinion.

Pressures from 'the centre'

Several sentencers complained about being given 'mixed messages' on sentencing both from politicians and from the senior judiciary. It was argued that not only do the Home Office, Lord Chancellor's Department and Lord Chief Justice often contradict each other, but that there are also inconsistencies in what is said *within* departments. It can be very difficult, one magistrate said, when the Government talks about being tough on crime, and "we are then told in the next breath – don't send anybody to prison." A Crown Court judge, similarly, commented:

> *One minute they're shouting because you're not being hard enough with them ... and the Court of Appeal are increasing sentences, and then they're telling us we shouldn't send people to jail.*

Some of the sentencers talked also of there being too much political interference in sentencing, or of tendencies on the part of Government to make 'knee-jerk reactions' as it seeks to influence the courts for cynical political gain. Magistrates in one focus group argued that the judicial process should be a matter of "justice, not popular justice". There is also a tendency in Government, it was sometimes suggested, to look to sentencers to solve problems that are actually well beyond their remit or capacity. A magistrate argued that if they are concerned about the size of the prison population, Government must look at the extent of violent crime rather than "blame those who administer the law". Likewise a district judge remarked that the prison population is determined by the extent of offending: "It's not us being capricious – which is what you often hear."

Thus, many sentencers appear to have a sense that current efforts by Government to reverse the rise in the prison population are poorly thought through, and are not backed up by the kind of political will and leadership that would be required to make them a success. This viewpoint was succinctly expressed by a senior judge:

> *The question for [Government] is pretty clear: do you really want to bring down the prison population – I mean, do you actually want to do it as opposed to want to say that you'll do it? [his emphasis]*

Pressures from the media and the public

Sentencing decisions are carried out in the public eye, and often arouse a great deal of interest among the public. Therefore, just as sentencers feel under pressure (or under contradictory pressures) from Government, they also feel pressure from the public since they are aware that their work is being constantly appraised by local and national media and ordinary people. Several of the sentencers, particularly district judges and magistrates, talked of being criticised by the media or the public for not being tough enough with the offenders who come before them. Criticisms come indirectly through the media but can also be felt directly by sentencers: one senior judge said that when he is at any kind of social event, if people find out that he is a judge they will all tell him that he is too lenient. A magistrate commented in the questionnaire that "my friends think that our sentences are woefully lenient".

According to many of the sentencers, there is particular scepticism among the public about the value of community penalties, which are typically viewed as a 'soft option' or 'cop out.' This point was vigorously expressed in a majority of the magistrates' focus groups. However, the magistrates' perceptions of public attitudes to community penalties are not entirely borne out by survey research on the topic (see Roberts et al., 2003; Roberts and Hough, 2002). Findings from a recent MORI poll are worth quoting in some detail. As many as 77% of respondents believed that probation could be a more effective alternative than prison for some offences; and 56% thought the Probation Service was effective at rehabilitating offenders. Less positively, however, 55% of respondents felt that probation was not effective at punishing offenders (supporting the magistrates' perception that the public view community penalties as 'soft'), and 48% that probation was out of touch with the public (National Probation Service, 2002).

While the magistrates and some of the other sentencers spoke of the public's tendency to be dismissive of community sentences, they indicated that this in itself would not discourage their use of such penalties. One striking exception to this, however, was provided by a senior judge who said that:

> *The one factor that would influence me in not imposing a probation order is the public perception of it, and therefore the Government or the authorities are going to have to sell it to the public as the hard option.*

A common theme in much of what sentencers (from senior judges to magistrates) said about public attitudes to sentencing was that many of these attitudes are uninformed – thanks to the selective or emotive reporting of court cases in both local and national media. Public views on sentencing, said one recorder, are based on misrepresentations of the facts by newspapers. A magistrate commented that if you buy the evening paper on your way home from court, you might find yourself hard-pressed to recognise its account of a case you dealt with earlier in the day. Two-thirds of respondents to the magistrates' questionnaire did not agree with the statement that the local media carry an accurate picture of local sentencing.

Some sentencers were aware that when people were confronted with the full details of a particular case, their sentencing preferences were not especially severe. Some of the magistrates, for example, noted that local people who take part in mock trials – held to inform the public about the criminal justice system – tend to soften considerably in their attitudes when confronted with realistic situations. As one magistrate put it:

> *We don't know what it is, you see they tell us that they think we're too soft and yet when you ask them to make the decision [at mock trials] they don't want to imprison.*

This tendency was also remarked upon by some of the judges and recorders, who referred to the findings of research in this field.[51] In general, there was strong support among the sentencers for measures to educate the public about all aspects of sentencing: for example,

---

51 The most probable points of reference, directly or indirectly, are Hough and Roberts (1998, 1999) and subsequent similar analyses of British Crime Survey findings.

many of the magistrates discussed the benefits of programmes such as 'Magistrates in the Community' which organise public talks and hold court open days.

Responding to the pressures

Unsurprisingly, given the intensity and conflicting nature of the political and social pressures upon them, sentencers did not appear to respond in a uniform way to these pressures. All recognised in various ways that they had a duty to the public, in that they should dispense justice in accordance with general views of what is and is not acceptable behaviour, and what is and is not proportionate punishment (in addition to other crucial concerns including public protection and the rehabilitation of offenders). But the sentencers varied in terms of how, precisely, they perceived and sought to discharge this public duty. It is evident that they deployed – singly or in various combinations – a range of different strategies to help them to gauge and fulfil their obligations to wider society. Seven strategies – suggested by the sentencers – emerged from the interviews and focus groups and are outlined below:

- *View legislation and/or guideline cases as the reflection of the general will of society, and hence as the overriding source of legitimacy for sentencing decisions*

  A district judge, for example, stated that her role was to represent public opinion as reflected in legislation; and a senior judge observed that 'Parliament represents the democratic voice …. Every judge recognises that.' Others said that public opinion is, rightly, reflected in guideline cases which in turn shape further sentencing decisions. One recorder, however, sharply dissented from this point of view, arguing that while Parliament sets out the parameters for sentencing, as it should, guideline cases are not justified because 'it's not for the judges or a body of judges to tell us how to sentence.'

- *Take account of victims (but, perhaps, not too much account)*

  Some sentencers spoke of having a special responsibility to the victims of the crimes they deal with. To ignore victims is to risk tempting 'people to take the law into their own hands' said one Crown Court judge. A magistrate noted that 'we have to think hard and long about the victims: that's part of our remit.' Another judge, however, spoke of how he took great care in one particular case to avoid being over-influenced by the presence of the victim in court.

- *Pay special attention to local concerns and issues*

  Several of the magistrates and one of the district judges said that it is important for them to take into account concerns about prevalent local crimes and, where necessary, to impose harsh penalties as a deterrent. Others, however, paid little attention to local circumstances.

- *Treat public opinion as one, but not the most important, factor in the balance of a sentencing decision*

  It was not uncommon for sentencers to talk of public opinion having a role, but a necessarily limited role, in sentencing decisions. For example, it was suggested that public opinion should 'inform' but not 'constrain' sentencing (senior judge); that it "is something we can't ignore, but [shouldn't] be the be-all and the end-all" (Crown Court judge); that a sentencer should consider public opinion but not be 'swayed' by it (district judge); that public opinion is a small but not a major factor – as "you try to make decisions that will be consistent with the public support for the criminal justice system" (district judge). This kind of approach is reflected also in the notion – voiced by a few of the sentencers – that it is important for them to be aware of but not necessarily influenced by the views of those around them.

- *Make sentencing decisions with regard to reasonable but not hysterical public opinion*

  Some sentencers who talked of public opinion as having a limited role in sentencing made a distinction between reasonable and unreasonable attitudes. A recorder commented that a sentencer should appreciate the views of the public, "but not tailor decisions to the editor of the Sun's cries". Another recorder, similarly, said that sentencers should be aware of the public mood but not be 'mob-driven'; while a Crown Court judge said he takes public opinion into account, "but I'm talking about reasonable public opinion now – I'm not talking about baying newspapers". A magistrate commented, in the questionnaire, that "*informed* concerns should be a factor taken into account when sentencing" [emphasis added].

- *Explain sentencing decisions so they can be understood – even by those who disagree with them*

  The importance of explaining sentences was stressed by a few of the sentencers, including a district judge who said, "I work on the basis that I always explain what I'm doing and if I can't explain it in a way that satisfies then perhaps I've got it wrong." Another district judge pointed out that "if you're giving a sentence that seems extraordinary, you're trained to justify it". In describing one of his cusp cases, a Crown Court judge said that he had to do "a lot of explaining" to the local press regarding his decision not to sentence to custody a woman convicted of large-scale VAT fraud.

- *Recognise that as a member of the public yourself, you act on behalf of the public*

  A recorder argued that he does not feel there is a need to take public opinion into account when making a decision "because I like to think that I'm part of that public, and I know more than the public because I'm told the surrounding circumstances". This viewpoint was expressed most frequently by magistrates. Their comments included: "The strength of the magistracy is that we are people of the people and that we're in touch with the people" and "JPs are members of the local public and are appointed to deliver 'local justice'" (questionnaire response).

An implicit or explicit aspect of all the above strategies was the assumption that, as a sentencer, it is necessary at times to distance oneself from the demands and expectations of politicians, the media and the general public. Many of the sentencers asserted their capacity to resist pressure: for example, by commenting in relation to certain cusp cases they "went out on a limb" in making a decision. One Crown Court judge pointed out that "We're here as judges, we're not here to be some kind of spokesmen of the electorate"; and another remarked:

> *If I pass a sentence and the local newspaper or a national newspaper get hold of it and starts slating me, well as far as I'm concerned it's water off a duck's back.*

A number of sentencers spoke about the particular difficulties associated with sentencing those accused of causing death by dangerous driving. These cases evidently crystallise many issues relating to sentencing and the role of public opinion. The offence of death by dangerous driving has been receiving increasingly severe sentences in recent years: the Criminal Justice Act 1993 responded to public pressure by increasing the maximum sentence from five to 10 years; and Government has recently proposed increasing the maximum further, to 14 years.[52] At the time of writing, the Court of Appeal had recently issued a guideline judgement, *Cooksley*,[53] in which it was stated that 12 to 18 months was an appropriate starting point, but that more serious contested cases might merit four or five years. Many sentencers seemed to resist the pressures to impose the most severe penalties, as it is an offence that (as one respondent pointed out) revolves around the consequences of an act rather than the intention.

Several of the judges and recorders talked of 'draconian' public attitudes to this offence, and of the difficulty of passing sentence when "you've got the public gallery full of relatives of the deceased" or when you know that the local news that evening will show "the next of kin talking about the price of life". A senior judge commented that his "biggest regret" was over a six-month sentence he once imposed for death by dangerous driving. He felt in hindsight that he should have used a non-custodial penalty; however he opted for custody because "I was scared of what the world would say". In contrast, a recorder indicated that in her view it was quite appropriate that, when passing sentence in a similar case, she had been influenced by the presence of the deceased's widow, in a wheelchair, in court. A district judge spoke at some length about his experience of sentencing a case of driving without due care (an offence for which he did not have the option of using custody) which had resulted in the deaths of five young men. He said that when he came to pass sentence:

> *I wrote down every word I was going to say before I went in, and despite the fact that I could only fine him and disqualify him I got not a murmur of abuse from the back. There I had to be very conscious of the fact that if I said something out of place or passed a sentence that not only [the families] didn't agree with but they didn't understand that there'd have been uproar.*

---

52 For more on the sentencing of causing death by dangerous driving see the Sentencing Advisory Panel Advice on its website (www.sentencing-advisory-panel.gov.uk).

53 R v Cooksley, 2 April 2003.

7 Conclusions – Reducing the prison population

This report has presented a wide range of findings about trends in sentencing practice and about the ways that sentencing decisions are made. This concluding chapter looks at the implications of these findings for ways of bringing down the prison population.

There are several policy options open to a Government confronted with a rapidly rising prison population. Not all involve attempts to contain or reverse the growth. Investing in more prisons is one obvious choice. This report has not tried to adjudicate between the options. Rather, the starting point of the study was the assumption that politicians who wish to curb the use of imprisonment in this country need to know the most promising ways of doing so.

Previous chapters have shown that the rise in the prison population can be attributed to various, interrelated factors. Sentencing practice has undoubtedly become more severe, reflecting (and reinforcing) a tougher legal and legislative framework of sentencing, and a more punitive social and political climate. It is also likely that some changes in patterns of offending, and particularly sentencers' *perceptions* that offending behaviour has changed for the worse, have encouraged greater use of custody.

Success in bringing down the prison population is hence dependent on changes to sentencing practice and the context in which sentencing is carried out. More specifically, policies targeting the prison population should relate to three levels of intervention:

- Adjustment to the legal and legislative framework of sentencing, to bring down custody rates and/or sentence length;

- Extending or improving the range of sentencing options, to persuade sentencers of the value of community penalties and other non-custodial penalties such as fines.

- Softening of the climate of political and public opinion on crime and punishment, so that sentencers feel at liberty to make more sparing use of custody, and greater use of the alternatives to custody.

The findings of this study offer insights into how such policy interventions might have most effect. Building on these insights, this chapter will discuss each level of intervention in turn.

Changing the legal and legislative framework

Changes to the legal and legislative framework are likely to have the most direct and tangible impact on sentencing. What is required here is a reversal of recent trends towards toughening up sentencing practice through legislation and guideline cases. One option is to focus on the decision whether or not to imprison, and another is to focus on subsequent decisions about sentence length.

The sentencers in this study were adamant that they used custody as an absolute last resort: that is, only when the seriousness of an offence or the lamentable record of an offender made it – in their eyes – inevitable. Thus they are not driven towards custody by lack of confidence in the non-custodial alternatives, or by any great faith in the intrinsic value of short sentences.

This commitment to custody as the last resort suggests that it will be difficult and risky to raise the custody threshold (the level of seriousness at which custody is used) through legislative moves or the use of guideline cases. Certainly it might be possible to take a small number of specific crime categories out of the custody bracket – but it is not easy to identify contenders for this. In the past this sort of adjustment has been made – albeit in an upward direction – for serious sexual offences for example, and for causing death by dangerous driving. However, an across-the-board change would certainly meet with considerable resistance from sentencers.

There is more scope for influencing sentence length. Some Crown Court judges described decisions about length of sentence both as easier than the 'in-out' decision, and as more amenable to direction. As discussed in Chapter 3, sentence length has been pushed up by legislation and by guideline judgements over the past decade, and in principle, reversals of such policy are possible. There are obviously political risks in doing so in terms of popular or media opposition – though probably less than the risks in trying to raise the custody threshold. Nevertheless, if there is genuine political will to restrict prison numbers, this provides the surest way of doing so. An initiative on any scale would demand a mix of legislation and guidance from the Court of Appeal and the new Sentencing Guidelines Council.

Given its focus on cusp cases, this study paid little attention to issues of sentence length other than with respect to short sentences; it can tell us little about how sentencers would respond to legislative moves to bring down sentence length across the board. However, there were some indications that respondents would be broadly supportive of such change. As regards short sentences, it seems likely that sentencers would largely agree with the principle of keeping these as short as possible. Keeping short custodial sentences very short would not compromise the main functions that these are believed to serve: that is, marking the gravity of an offence, and deterring relatively inexperienced offenders through the 'clang of the prison gates'.

At the time of writing, the Criminal Justice Bill before Parliament included provision for a new short custodial sentence with supervision on release ('Custody Plus'). The idea was attractive to sentencers in this study, and properly implemented it could play a significant part in bringing down the length of short sentences. However, there is a real risk that it will be used *not* for offenders who currently receive sentences of six to 12 months, but for those who get community penalties. The effects of this kind of 'net-widening' could be to push up, rather than bring down, the prison population.[54]

Extending and improving non-custodial penalties

The main non-custodial penalties fall into two groups, community penalties – CPOs, CROs, related forms of community supervision – and fines. This study can say more about the former than the latter, though it became clear towards the end of the study that strategies to resuscitate the use of fines could play an important part in containing the prison population.

Strengthening community penalties

One longstanding strategy for restricting prison numbers has been to strengthen the range and rigour of community orders. In the 1980s and early 1990s the then Conservative Government aimed to develop 'punishment in the community' and this commitment to

---

54 Note that the introduction of Detention and Training Orders for young offenders may have had a net-widening effect (see Hazel *et al.*, 2002).

'toughen up' probation has continued to the present. There may well be a need to improve the public face of probation work, but an important conclusion from this study is that offering sentencers a wider and more attractive menu of community penalties will not be, in itself, an effective way to discourage them from using custody.

Chapter 5 documented a general satisfaction with the range and content of existing community sentences. Sentencers insisted that they use community sentences whenever it is appropriate for a case: in other words, that they do not use custody because of perceived weaknesses in or lack of community options. In only two out of the 150 custodial cusp cases cited by the sentencers was it said that the custodial sentence was passed for want of an adequate alternative.

There is now considerable experience in the development of community alternatives to imprisonment. England and Wales has one of the most developed probation services in the world, with a wide range of community options. The experience in Britain and the United States of providing community penalties as alternative to custody has often been disappointing, with two kind of emergent problems (Morris and Tonry, 1991). The first is that properly enforced community orders are likely to have a high failure rate amongst the high-risk offenders facing short prison sentences, with high rates of imprisonment following breach. The second problem is that the very attractiveness of these sentences leads sentencers to use them not for offenders facing imprisonment but for offenders who would previously have received less elaborate community penalties or simply a fine. Morgan (2002) has referred to the Probation Service as 'silted up' with such offenders to an extent that jeopardizes the Service's capacity.

However, while the scope for reducing use of custody by extending community alternatives may be limited, maintaining and (wherever possible) improving sentencer confidence in community options should be regarded as a crucial component of any wider strategy to restrict prison numbers. There are three main ways in which this can be achieved.

First, improvements could be made to the provision, organisation and management of that small group of community penalties which can, in the view of sentencers, serve as genuine alternatives to imprisonment. Most notably, an extension in provision of Drug Treatment and Testing Orders – which were widely welcomed by sentencers as tough penalties which enable some offenders to take major steps towards rehabilitation – could play an important part here. Additionally, as sentencers become more knowledgeable about curfew orders, these may increasingly be viewed as suitable alternatives to short-term prison sentences for many offenders. For such penalties to achieve their greatest impact, however, it is essential that they are explicitly targeted at those who would otherwise go to prison, and not (as, it appears, has often happened in the past) at those who could perfectly well be fined or given a conventional community penalty.

Secondly, enhancing sentencer confidence in community options may depend on better funding and staffing of the Probation Service and of other providers of community penalties. This study found ample evidence that while most sentencers believe probation provides a generally good service, they are also concerned that this service is hampered in various respects by a lack of resources. It seems unlikely that levels of confidence in probation will be retained for any length of time if sentencers continue to have a sense of a strained and underfunded organisation. If these are misperceptions they obviously need to be corrected; it is more likely that sentencers' assessments are accurate, and that the remedy is extra money.

A third way of raising the credibility of community penalties in the eyes of sentencers may be to develop and extend the review process that applies at present only to DTTOs.[55] This process entails regular appearances before the court by the offender who is on the order, to allow progress to be monitored. As was discussed in Chapter 5, sentencers generally warmed to the notion of a more personal contract between the judge or magistrates and the offender. The review process is by no means cheap, and it can create serious listing problems. If it does prove possible to engender a keener sense of responsibility to the court amongst offenders, this could enhance the effectiveness of the orders in question.

Resuscitating fines as a sentencing option

Chapter 2 described how the use of the fine has shrunk by nearly a third over the last 10 years. In the 1970s fines accounted for over half of sentences for indictable offences.[56] In 1991 the figure was 35%. In 2001 they accounted for 24% of the total. Chapter two suggested that community penalties have substituted for fines.

The decline of the fine has affected the size of the prison population indirectly, but this indirect impact may be substantial. It will be remembered from Chapter 4 that sentencers talked in terms of prison as a sentence of last resort, used only when all the other options have been exhausted. Failure to respond to previous community penalties was often cited as evidence that the offender had 'reached the end of the road'. To pursue this metaphor, extending the use of fines may serve as a form of road-building that at best deflects an offender entirely from further offending without resort to imprisonment, and at worst defers the point in their criminal career where prison becomes inevitable. There would be the added benefit of relieving pressure on the Probation Service, increasing the chances of success with the smaller number of offenders who they would be supervising.

As was mentioned earlier, the use of fines was not the focus of this research, and fines were discussed only incidentally in focus groups and interviews. The findings offer only a little guidance on how the use of fines might be encouraged. Clearly sentencers will need to have more confidence that if they impose a fine, it will actually get paid. There are two issues to focus on. First it would make sense to revisit the idea of 'unit fines' introduced by the 1991 Criminal Justice Act, which related the size of fines to offenders' incomes. Unit fine schemes operate effectively in many European countries, and the unit fine pilots in this country were successful (Moxon *et al.*, 1990). However the idea was so poorly implemented in 1992 that politicians have shied away from the principle ever since. An effective scheme would improve substantially levels of compliance with fines. Secondly, there needs to be a thorough re-examination of the enforcement options for those offenders who do actually fail to pay their fines. As emerged from some of the magistrates' focus groups, different courts have widely differing success rates in securing compliance, and it should be possible for those with the worst records to learn from those with the best.

The climate of opinion about crime and punishment

This report has paid considerable attention to arguments about the climate of opinion within which sentencers operate. Along with many other industrialized liberal democracies, this

---

55 Though the Custody Minus provisions in the Criminal Justice Bill include a review process.

56 For both male and female offenders, aged 18 or over.

country has been developing increasingly punitive penal policies, fuelled by public and media concerns about crime. This results in real pressures on sentencers, who sometimes feel unable to take the decisions they feel are right, including use of non-custodial options, without fear of media and public condemnation.

Many of the sentencers who participated in this study spoke of their ability to resist pressures from the media and the public, and of the critical importance of being able to do so. However, they emphasised also their conviction that they have a duty to the public to ensure that their sentencing decisions reflect and reinforce the norms of wider society. Sentencing can thus become a difficult – and ambiguous – balancing act of, for example, ensuring that decisions are 'informed' by public opinion but not 'constrained' by it; or taking into account 'reasonable' public opinion while not allowing oneself to be 'mob-driven'.

The reasons for the evolution of the current mood of populist punitiveness are many and complex. Several commentators have identified characteristics of 'late-modern' society that have both engendered popular attachment to simple and tough solutions to crime and have led politicians to attach greater weight to this 'public voice' than hitherto (e.g. Bottoms, 1995; Roberts et al., 2003; Ryan, 2003). Social and technological change has left us bereft of traditional certainties and sources of trust. Family life, certainty of employment and religious belief no longer occupy the same social space as they did half a century ago. These wide-ranging insecurities that people feel in the face of rapid social change may be translated into concerns about the risks of crime and about threats to personal safety. 'Criminals' become society's whipping boys; and the criminal justice system becomes the whip.

Another consequence of life in a rapidly changing and less controllable world is that there is less public confidence in public institutions, including the criminal justice system. In response to this shift in public mood, liberal democracies have abandoned traditionally paternalistic political styles in favour of more obviously responsive or populist ones.

At the same time, mass-media representations – or mis-representations – of crime and justice have systematically misinformed the public, and encouraged politicians to respond to the sense of public anger about crime that they have fuelled. The extent of public ignorance about crime and justice is now well documented. People tend to over-estimate the severity of crime problems and to underestimate the severity of court sentences. It is unsurprising, therefore, that they have little confidence in the criminal process. However, politicians have tended to respond to public disquiet with rhetoric about tough-minded action against offenders; much more rarely have they adopted the politically risky strategy of explaining the realities of current sentencing practice to the electorate. The result is that the climate of opinion about punishment becomes more heated, and sentencers respond to these changes.

Whether it is possible to halt or reverse these processes is hard to say. The levers through which Government can exercise control over its own institutions are weak enough. Changing popular perceptions and public mood is much harder – especially when the mass media's handling of crime is implicated in the problem. However, there may be enough points of leverage to limit the reach of political populism into sentencing policy.

Sentencers, penal reformers and their academic allies need to learn from their failure to make any significant impact on penal debate when penal populism emerged so clearly in Britain in the mid 1990s. On the one hand they need to use social marketing techniques more effectively to convey clearly messages about crime and punishment. On the other hand, any such social marketing has to be scrupulously honest if it is to maintain any long-term authority.

Certainly there is a pressing need to improve the quality of information available to the public about crime and justice. But those best placed to do so – government researchers and statisticians – have increasingly less credibility in a world which equates Government with spin. Whilst the technical quality and integrity of Home Office research and statistics remains high, any attempt by Government to reassure the public will elicit a sceptical response. This puts a particular obligation on reform groups and on criminologists to tackle public misperceptions. It is also important to ensure that the political costs of penal populism are increased. Where politicians put forward popular but flawed proposals, those proposals need to be exposed as flawed by people who command credibility and authority. Finally, politicians need to be offered more cogent and compelling alternative models of crime control.

These proposals are easy to list, but hard to implement. If they are to be given any practical reality, professionals within and around the criminal process need to think harder about the institutional arrangements needed to ensure that there are adequate buffers between penal practice and populist policy. We need more effective alliances between practitioners, academics and reform groups that allow rational penal policy to develop a coherent, audible and authoritative voice. In the absence of such alliances, the likelihood is that populist attachment to prison as a solution to crime will continue to dominate penal reform.

The political will to restrict prison numbers

The problems of a rapidly surging prison population have been with us since the early 1990s.[57] Politicians of all hues have been anxious to address the problem, but not so anxious as to risk media and popular criticism for being 'soft on crime'. The sense that sentencers in this study had of 'mixed messages' coming from central Government was marked. The ways that sentencing practice and the climate of opinion about punishment are interlaced suggest that no real progress will be made unless there is unequivocal political leadership in pursuing changes in both the former and the latter.

The surest way to restrict prison numbers in the short term is legislation or sentencing guidance to raise the custody threshold and to shorten the length of prison sentences. But this strategy will fail in the long term if it is not accompanied by determined action to reduce the temperature of political and public debate about crime and punishment. This report has suggested that there is a vicious circle in which public anxieties about crime and punishment trigger political responses that inflame rather than calm these anxieties, and prompt sentencers to pass tougher sentences. What is needed are ways of reversing the cycle, so that initiatives to change the climate of opinion about crime and punishment interact with and support changes in the legal and legislative sentencing framework and measures to strengthen community penalties.

---

57 Concern about the rising prison population was evident long before then, but those who were preoccupied about prison numbers in the 1980s never envisaged at that time increases on the scale seen in the 1990s.

References

Ashworth, A. (2002) 'Robbery Re-assessed', *Criminal Law Review*, November 2002, pp851-72.

Ashworth, A. and Hough, M. (1996) Sentencing and the Climate of Opinion, *Criminal Law Review*, November, pp761-848.

Audit Commission (2002) *Changing Habits: The Commissioning and Management of Drug Treatment Services for Adults*, Briefing February 2002, London: Audit Commission.

Ayres, M. and colleagues (2000) *Cautions, Court Procedure and Sentencing England and Wales 1999*. Home Office Statistical Bulletin Issue 19/00. London: Home Office.

Bennett, T., Holloway, K. and Williams, T. (2001) *Drug Use and Offending: Summary Results from the First Year of the NEW-ADAM Research Programme*, Home Office Research Findings 148, London: Home Office

Blunkett, D. (2001) Speech delivered to the National Probation Service inaugural conference, June 2001.

Bottoms, T. (1995) 'The Politics and Philosophy of Sentencing', in Clarkson, C. and Morgan, R. (eds.) *The Politics of Sentencing Reform*. Oxford: Clarendon Press.

Carlisle, Lord (Chairman) (1988) *The Parole System in England and Wales. Report of the Review Committee* (Cm 532). London: HMSO.

Corkery, J. (2002) *Drug Seizure and Offender Statistics, United Kingdom, 2000*. London: Home Office.

Davies, M. and Tyrer, J. (2003) '"Filling in the Gaps" – A Study of Judicial Culture', *Criminal Law Review*, April 2003, pp243-265.

Department of Health (2003) *Health Survey of England*. [http://www.doh.gov.uk/stats/trends1.htm].

Dodgson, K., Mortimer, E. and Sugg, D. (2000) *Assessing Prisoners for Home Detention Curfew: a guide for practitioners*. RDS Practitioners Guide 1. London: Home Office.

Dunbar, I. and Langdon, A. (1998) *Tough Justice: Sentencing and Penal Policies in the 1990s*, London: Blackstone.

Flood-Page, C. and Mackie, A. (1998) *Sentencing Practice: An Examination of Decisions in Magistrates' Courts and the Crown Court in the mid-1990s*, Home Office Research Study 180, London: Home Office.

Gelsthorpe, L. and Morris, A. (2002) 'Women's Imprisonment in England and Wales: A Penal Paradox', *Criminal Justice*, 2 (3), pp277-301.

Godfrey, C., Eaton, G. McDougall, C. and Culyer, A. (2002) *The Economic and Social Costs of Class A Drug Use in England and Wales, 2000* Home Office Research Study 249, London: Home Office.

Goldblatt. P., and Lewis, C. (1998) *Reducing Offending: an assessment of research evidence on ways of dealing with offending behaviour.* Home Office Research Study 187, London: Home Office.

Hammersley, R., Marsland, L. and Reid, M. (2003) *Substance Use by Young Offenders*, Home Office Research Findings 192, London: Home Office.

Hazel, N., Hagell, A., Liddle, M., Archer, D., Grimshaw, R. and King, J. (2002) *Assessment of the Detention and Training Order and its Impact on the Secure Estate across England and Wales.* London: Youth Justice Board.

Hedderman, C. (2003) 'Why are more women being sentenced to custody?' In McIvor, G. (ed.) *Women Who Offend.* Jessica Kingsley.

Hedderman, C., Ellis, T. and Sugg, D. (1999) *Increasing Confidence in Community Sentences: The Results of Two Demonstration Projects*, Home Office Research Study 194, London: Home Office.

Hedderman, C. and Moxon, D. (1992) *Magistrates' court or Crown Court? Mode of trial decisions and sentencing.* Home Office Research Study 125, London: Home Office.

Henham, R. (1996) 'Truth in sentencing: Some problems of enforcement strategy', *Web Journal of Current Legal Issues*, 1996 (Issue 3). [http://www.webjcli.ncl.ac.uk/1996/issue3/henham3.htm].

HM Prisons (2003) Statistics – prison population, 2 May 03 [www.hmprisonservice.gov.uk/statistics].

Home Office (1992) *Criminal Statistics England and Wales 1991*, London: HMSO.

Home Office (1993) *Prison Statistics England and Wales 1991*, London: HMSO.

Home Office (1997) *Section 49 of The Criminal Procedure and Investigations Act 1996 and Section 51 of The Crime (Sentences) Act 1997.* Home Office Circular 45/1997. London: Home Office.

Home Office (2001) *Making Punishments Work: Report of a Review of the Sentencing Framework for England and Wales* ('The Halliday Report'), London: Home Office.

Home Office (2002a) *Criminal Statistics England and Wales 2001*, London: TSO.

Home Office (2002b) *Home Office Statement in Response to the Prison Population Projections*, 9 December 2002.

Home Office (2002c) *Probation Statistics England and Wales 2001.* London: Home Office.

Home Office (2003) *Prison Statistics England and Wales 2001*, London: TSO.

Hood, R. and Shute, S. (2000) *The Parole System at Work: a study of risk based decision-making.* Home Office Research Study 202. London: Home Office.

Hough, M. (1996) *Problem Drug Use and Criminal Justice: a review of the literature. Drugs Prevention Initiative paper No. 15.* London: Home Office Central Drugs Prevention Unit.

Hough, M., McSweeney T. and Turnbull, P. (2002) *Drugs and Crime: what are the links? Evidence to the Home Affairs Committee Inquiry into drug policy.* London: DrugScope.

Hough, M. and Roberts, J. (1998) *Attitudes to Punishment: findings from the 1996 British Crime Survey*. Home Office Research Study 179, London: Home Office.

Hough, M. and Roberts, J. (1999) 'Sentencing Trends in Britain: Public Knowledge and Public Opinion', *Punishment and Society*, Vol 1, 1. pp11-26.

Hoyle, C., Young, R. and Hill, R (2002) *Proceed with Caution: an evaluation of the Thames Valley Police initiative in restorative cautioning*. York: York Publishing Services.

Levenson, J. (2002) *Prison Overcrowding: the Inside Story*. London: Prison Reform Trust.

Lloyd, C. and Walmsley, R. (1989) *Changes in Rape Offences and Sentencing*, Home Office Research Study 105, London: Home Office.

Magistrates' Association (2000) *Sentencing Guidelines*. London: Magistrates' Association.

Mair, G. and Mortimer, E. (1996) *Curfew Orders with Electronic Monitoring: An Evaluation of the First Twelve Months of Trials in Greater Manchester, Norfolk and Berkshire, 1995-96*, Home Office Research Study 163, London: Home Office.

MHA Matrix and Nacro (2003) *Evaluation of drug testing in the criminal justice system in nine pilot areas*. Findings 180. London: Home Office.

Miers, D. (2001) *An International Review of Restorative Justice*. Home Office Crime Reduction Research Series Paper 10. London: Home Office.

Miers, D., Maguire, M., Goldie, S., Sharpe, K., Hale, C., Netten, A., Uglow, S., Doolin, K., Hallam, A., Enterkin, J. and Newburn, T. (2001) *An Evaluation of Restorative Justice Schemes*. Home Office Crime Reduction Research Series Paper 9. London: Home Office.

Morgan, R. (2003) 'Thinking about the Demand for Probation Services', *Probation Journal*, 50 (1), pp7-19.

Morris, N. and Tonry, M. (1991) *Between Prison and Probation: Intermediate Punishment in a Rational Sentencing System*. New York: Oxford University Press.

Moxon, D., Sutton, M. and Hedderman, C. (1990) *Unit fines: experiments in four courts*. Research and Planning Unit Paper 59. London: Home Office.

National Probation Service (2002) *Perceptions of the National Probation Service – Results of the telephone survey DRAFT*. A research study conducted by MORI for the National Probation Service. London: National Probation Service.

Parker, H. Sumner, M. and Jarvis, G. (1989) *Unmasking the Magistrates: The 'custody or not' decision in sentencing young offenders*, Milton Keynes: Open University Press.

Parole Board (1994) *Report of the Parole Board for 1993* (HC 450). London: HMSO.

Prime, J. (2002) *Progress made against Home Office Public Service Agreement Target 10*. Home Office Online Report 16/02. [www.homeoffice.gov.uk/rds].

Richardson, A., Budd, T., Engineer, R., Phillips, A., Thompson, J. and Nicholls, J. (2003) *Drinking, Crime and Disorder*, Home Office Research Findings 185, London: Home Office.

Roberts, J. and Hough, M. (eds) (2002) *Changing Attitudes to Punishment: Public opinion, crime and justice.* Cullompton: Willan Publishing.

Roberts, J.V., Stalans, L.S., Indermaur, D. and Hough, M. (2003) *Penal Populism and Public Opinion. Findings from Five Countries.* New York: Oxford University Press.

Ryan, M. (2003) *Penal Policy and Political Culture in England and Wales.* Winchester: Waterside Press.

Simmons, J. and colleagues (2002) *Crime in England and Wales 2001/2.* Home Office Statistical Bulletin 7/02. London: Home Office.

Tonry, M. and Frase, R. (2001) *Sentencing and Sanctions in Western Countries.* Oxford: Oxford University Press.

TSO (The Stationery Office) (2002) *Justice for All.* CM 5563. London: TSO.

Turnbull, P., McSweeney, T., Webster, R., Edmunds, M. and Hough, M. (2000) *Drug Treatment and Testing Orders: final evaluation report,* Home Office Research Study 212. London: Home Office.

Von Hirsch, A., Bottoms, A. E., Burney, E. and Wikström, P-O. (1999). *Criminal Deterrence and Sentencing Severity: An analysis of recent research.* Oxford: Hart.

Walmsley, R. (2003) *World Prison Population List (fourth edition),* Home Office Research Findings 188, London: Home Office.

Walter, I. (2002) *Evaluation of the national roll-out of curfew orders,* Home Office Online Report 15/02, London: Home Office.

Walter, I. Sugg, D. and Moore, L. (2001) *A Year on the Tag: interviews with criminal justice practitioners and electronic monitoring staff about curfew orders,* Home Office Research Findings 140, London: Home Office.

Woolf, Lord (2001) *Restorative Justice,* Speech to the Youth Justice Board, Church House Conference Centre, London, 25 October 2001.

Woolf, Lord (2002) *Achieving Criminal Justice,* the 2nd Rose Lecture, Manchester Town Hall, 29 October 2002.

Youth Justice Board (2002) *Annual Review 2001/2,* London: Youth Justice Board.